Mikey
Go Bronz
River Knight

MW01488123

The Wrong Man Out.

Kenneth J. Ratajczak, M.D.

authorHOUSE®

AuthorHouse™
1663 Liberty Drive, Suite 200
Bloomington, IN 47403
www.authorhouse.com
Phone: 1-800-839-8640

First published by AuthorHouse 4/7/2008

ISBN: 978-1-4343-5678-9 (sc)
ISBN: 978-1-4343-5679-6 (hc)

Library of Congress Control Number: 2008900763

Printed in the United States of America
Bloomington, Indiana

This book is printed on acid-free paper.

Dedication

I dedicate this book to:
the memory of "Shoeless" Joe (Joseph Jefferson) Jackson;
my wife, Anne, who has listened to my whining about the unfair
treatment that "Shoeless" Joe has received, and the many hours on
airplanes that I spent reading about Joe rather than talking to her;
my children, Kevin and Laura, who have put up with my whining,
also;
my grandchildren, Madison and, especially, Kyle, my grandson who
my son and daughter-in-law refused to name Joseph Jefferson over
my incessant lobbying. I forgive them because Kyle is a beautiful
grandson…who I will try to get to emulate Joe Jackson's swing, what
a beautiful swing.
Sorry, Joe, I guess I should have had this work done before Kyle was
born. Let's see if we can get you reinstated and into Major League
Baseball and then into the Major League Baseball Hall of Fame.

Preface

I started this journey reading Harvey Frommer's book, *Shoeless Joe and Ragtime Baseball*. After a lot of the "facts" and stories started resurfacing in other books that I read, I reread the book to make sure that I wasn't misguided by my first impression of Joe Jackson from Frommer's book. I don't think that I was.

On November 10, 2006, as I was starting this work, I was watching an episode of the television series Numbers, the "Hard Ball" episode. This was the first time that I had watched this series. They began talking about sabermetrics, and how this type of statistical analysis showed that "Shoeless" Joe Jackson played the best that he could in the 1919 World Series. I turned to my wife and said, ""Shoeless" Joe Jackson is speaking to me. He wants me to take on this venture." I truly believe that "Shoeless" Joe Jackson spoke to me that night; chills ran across my body. I had to pursue this work.

I will start by stating that I am a Chicago White Sox fan and have been one since I was six years old. As a fan, my greatest thrill was the Sox winning the 2005 World Series. I went to spring training in Tucson before the 2005 campaign and was a bit discouraged, again, but that team came together and won it all! I attended Chicago White Sox Baseball Fantasy camp in January 2008, and I encourage anyone who has the ways and means to attend a fantasy camp if at all possible. The camaraderie with the campers and coaches and the chance to meet and talk baseball with some of the greats of the game is priceless.

And I remember the 1959 American League pennant race. I can still hear the play-by-play as I listened to my transistor radio under the covers in my bed as the White Sox clinched the pennant. Jerry Staley, the knuckleballer, comes in, in relief, with one out, ninth inning, a runner on first, and the White Sox leading six to four. "It's a ground ball to Aparicio, Aparicio to Fox, Fox to Kluszewski…a double play and the White Sox clinch the American League pennant!"

Of course, to a White Sox fan, the darkest time is the 1919 World Series. I am not going to try to prove that there wasn't a "fix". I am not even going to try to prove that "Shoeless" Joe Jackson was entirely without fault. What I am going to try to do is show that "Shoeless" Joe should be reinstated to Major League Baseball, and that there are two people in the Baseball Hall of Fame that are far less deserving than Joseph Jefferson Jackson, and those two people are the reason that Joe is not in the Hall of Fame. So if you want to accuse me of being biased, you are right, but I did try to uncover as much of the truth that could be uncovered. Not everything that I learned endeared me to the 1919 White Sox or even to "Shoeless" Joe even though I went into this biased in favor of "Shoeless" Joe.

Some of this will be a rehash of history, the times, and the circumstances surrounding the 1919 World Series, the "facts", and the conclusions, but I hope to present a new perspective, one that, to the best of my knowledge and research, has never been truly or completely explored: The wrong man out and the wrong men in.

I don't want to give baseball or any of the characters involved in the 1919 World Series scandal a black eye because I love baseball; I admire Joe Jackson, and I think he got a raw deal; and I feel that Major League Baseball is responsible, and they need to take the blame for their actions. Jackson is legendary and has had a major effect on the game of baseball. His swing has been emulated by many of the greats, Babe Ruth and Ted Williams, to mention two.

In 1999, after the new White Sox park was built, I had hoped that the Comiskeys would put the cards on the table, and, to honor "Shoeless" Joe, build a statue of him in front of the park. It didn't happen.

So, I want to thank the many authors and the mounds of research that they did to ease my burden by publishing their books and giving me access to the information that they were able to unearth. I want to thank them for their candid opinions and the arguments they presented to back their opinions.

Next, I want to thank Major League Baseball for being Major League Baseball, and I want to ask the commissioner to look at Joseph Jefferson Jackson through this work and his heart and not through the commissioners' hearts from Kenesaw Mountain Landis to today. Mr. Bud Selig, the present Commissioner, may have been the only commissioner who wanted to take an honest look at Joe Jackson but never got around to it or never made a statement as to his findings. I have written two letters to Mr. Selig presenting much of this evidence in support of Shoeless Joe, but all I got back was a couple of letters, probably from some staffer, with a bunch of nothing and an unwillingness to take another look at Shoeless Joe Jackson.

I would like to add a "thanks" to Ron Kittle, the 1983 American League Rookie of the Year, for plugging my book at the 2008 Chicago White Sox Fantasy Baseball Camp. I will need all the help that I can get since this is a self published book.

I would like to add a very special "thank you" to Scott Hudson who, after hearing me speak of this book, went on line and found pictures of Joe Jackson. Scott is a very talented, young artist who took the pictures that he found and created the picture of "Shoeless" Joe that adorns the cover of this book.

Finally, I will put Major League Baseball, Charles Comiskey, Kenesaw Mountain Landis, and Joe Jackson on a fictitious trial at the end of this book, and you are the Jury. I ask you to email Major League Baseball at mlb.com and tell them what your decision is. The decision that you, as the jury, are asked to answer is, "Should Joseph Jefferson Jackson be reinstated to Major League Baseball?" If so, it is not our decision, but Major League Baseball's to decide if "Shoeless" Joe should be inducted into the Hall of Fame.

With the "steroid scandal" coming to light, Major League Baseball has enough to deal with, but it sure seems like it tried to hide its head in the sand on this one, too. I certainly mean no malice toward Major League Baseball, but, since it would not open its mind, then I feel obligated to publish this work.

CHAPTER 1

"The Setting for the 1919 World Series and After."

The government ordered all horse racing suspended until the end of World War I. Gamblers looked for another outlet, and they began congregating in hotels where major league teams stayed. Gambling became endemic to baseball...open betting in the park was rife and more pronounced outside of them. Gambling and baseball had been allied since 1865 and maybe even 1860. The players saw gamblers run through baseball without anyone laying a glove on them.[1] The gamblers bragged about which player and which game they fixed. Chick Gandil, who was allegedly the centerpiece of the White Sox in the "fix" was friends with Sport Sullivan, a bookie and gambler with known connections with the mob. There supposedly was a telegram from Chick Gandil to his wife before the Series began: *I HAVE BET MY SHOES* (and maybe Joe Jackson's). Hence the name "Shoeless" Joe. But I digress. When the series was over, Gandil spent money very freely. "Baseball's contamination by business and gambling were regarded as minor but necessary evils in a supposedly free-market economy."[2] Baseball ignored the influence of gambling on baseball. Even some of the managers and owners were heavy gamblers and some owners had their hands in gambling ventures. John O. Seys, secretary of the Cubs, admitted that he had acted as stakeholder for several of Abe Attel's bets, as well as those for the Levi brothers, all of whom are tied with the gambling syndicates that were involved in the 1919 World Series "fix".

Prior to the start of the 1919 World Series, Cincinnati pitcher, Rod Heller, turned down a $5,000 bribe from an unknown source to throw a game. Cincinnati center fielder and leading hitter, Ed Roush, said, "The gamblers tried to work on our pitcher, Rod Heller, but he squelched them." Reds manager, Pat Moran, asked Heller outright if the gamblers approached him, and Heller said, "Sure did. Showed me five $1,000 bills if I'd make sure we lost today's game... I told him to get out of my sight. If I ever saw him again, I'd beat him up." Should Moran had been banned from baseball? He certainly knew about wrongdoing.

In 1865 three players from the New York Mutuals threw a game; in 1877 four Louisville players confessed to conspiring with gamblers; and in 1919 Hal Chase was accused of betting on a game and trying to bribe a teammate. Chase was acquitted and reinstated due to lack of evidence. "(Eliot) Asinof emphasizes that "baseball and betting were aligned from the beginning. The official, if unspoken, policy was to let the rottenness grow rather than risk the danger involved in exposure and cleanup…thus implicating the owners and the baseball establishment in what would eventually transpire. So all the investigations were squashed."[3] "Baseball had shown in the past its will to investigate was wanting. In 1919 that had not changed much."[4] The pattern of disciplinary action by baseball officialdom was a financial slap on the wrist, followed after a "decent interval" by reinstatement, if the players desired it, or at worst an unpublicized, graceful exit from the game.[5] Hugh Fullerton wrote, "So long as the gate receipts are more important than winning the game, there can be no real reform."[6] Even the incident that led to the grand jury investigation-the suspected throwing of the August 31 Cubs-Phillies game-was swept under the carpet. The National League investigated and cleared Buck Herzog of any wrong doing.

Another undercurrent of the times was anti-Semitism, and many of the gamblers and Arnold Rothstein, who was alleged to be the money behind the gamblers, a number of whom were Jewish, fed the reporters more fodder for their stories. History seems to suggest that Rothstein did not back the gamblers, and, to Rothstein's tragic death, he denied any connection with the "Big Fix." The gamblers all ran in close circles, and Rothstein, in one way or another associated with many of the shady characters tied to the "fix," and it is pretty certain that Rothstein knew about the fix and either he himself or figures close to him wagered big money on the 1919 World Series. Rothstein also "had it on good authority from his National League friends, Stoneham and McGraw [of the New York Giants], that [Pat] Moran [the Cincinnati Reds manager] had the better team in the Series.[7] Bill Maharg, a small time gambler, said that he and William "Sleepy" Burns met with Rothstein by appointment, but "Rothstein turned his back on the deal thinking that a fix of a World Series was not possible."

But there is a suggestion that Rothstein was behind the "fix." Allan Pinkerton [of the famous Pinkerton Investigation] "expressed to [Ban] Johnson his contention that Arnold Rothstein was the "prime mover" behind the fixers..."[8] Chick Gandil, in an interview in a 1956 *Sports Illustrated,* claimed to be the ring leader of the "Big Fix" and that he met Arnold Rothstein. Harold Seymour wrote that after Rothstein was shot to death, "affidavits were found in his files testifying to the fact that he paid out $80,000 for the World Series fix."[9] When the lid blew off the "Big Fix", Abe Attel's attorney, William Fallon "ordered Abe Attell to Montreal, Sport Sullivan to Mexico, and suggested that Rothstein and his wife should take a slow ocean liner to Europe...Arnold would pay for everything, including Fallon's fee..."[10] Ban Johnson, the baseball commissioner, in a public statement absolved Rothstein of all guilt. "In return for Johnson's public statement absolving him of all guilt, Rothstein would give Johnson the Polo Grounds."[11] Sleepy Burns "laid responsibility for the fix directly at the feet of Rothstein.[12] Edd Roush heard a gambler say, "It was fixed all right... A fellow named Zork came up with the idea, but the money came from New York, from Rothstein."[13] The FBI found affidavits in Rothstein's possession that told of Rothstein bribing the "Black Sox."

On September 23, 1920, New York Giants pitcher Rube Benton testified at a grand jury probe that a Cincinnati betting commissioner named Hahn told him that five White Sox players demanded $100,000 to throw the series, and that was paid to them by a group of Pittsburgh gamblers.[14] Rothstein's name, reputation, and apparent wealth were all the gamblers needed. The players were called Jewish dupes and gentile boobs. Abe Attell later bragged that he was the payoff man. And there probably was a "fix." Pat Moran, the Reds manager, had also stated that he knew that the gamblers tried to get his starting pitcher in game one, Heller, drunk. Why didn't Moran report this? Would his word have added credibility to the rumors of the "Fix"?

Just before the players were indicted, Bill Maharg told the newspapers that he was contacted by "Sleepy" Burns, and they met with Cicotte and Gandil, and Cicotte told Maharg that a group of prominent players on the White Sox would be willing to "throw" the World Series for $100,000.

After the players were indicted the case went to the grand jury, but the case was filled with problems. First, Hugo M Friend, the presiding judge instructed the jury that the state had to prove that the players' intent was to defraud the victims named in the indictment and the public, not merely to throw the World Series. The State's Attorney, Maclay Hoyne admitted that he was "uncertain whether any crime has been committed." Legal action was taken largely because the public demanded it.[15] To prove a conspiracy, there was a need to prove that there were bribes, and, after Arnold Rothstein, who was accused of fronting the money, was never subpoenaed, ..."the prosecutors relied on coerced confessions of a few ball players who had been intimidated." The confessions and immunity waivers then mysteriously disappeared from the state attorney's office--later to surface in Comiskey's possession.

It took the jury one ballot and 3 hours to acquit the players of all charges. There was joy and mass hysteria in the court room after the verdict was handed down. Some Chicagoans felt that the players were "gods" of baseball, although many people felt that they were uncouth toughs and hayseeds. Baseball players were thought to be little more than grownup boys.

The facts are all cloaked in mystery and have been run around the block more than once since the 1919 World Series. "Conflicting evidence, stories that changed from day to day, confessions that were later retracted, all muddy the water sufficiently to keep many of the exact details shrouded in a fog of mystery."[16] Even the news coverage was dubious since there are numerous accounts of the same plays in the 1919 World Series that read as if they were completely different events. Donald Gropema in *Say It Ain't So, Joe!: The True Story of Shoeless Joe Jackson and the 1919 World Series* differs with Asinof on whether Jackson attended a September 21, 1919 players' meeting to discuss the fix; whether he definitely joined the plot at the meeting; whether he later demanded $20,000 from Gandil to participate in the conspiracy; whether he told Gleason or Comiskey that he didn't want to play just prior to the first game; whether Lefty Williams gave Jackson $5,000 before the fifth game or after the series; and whether Jackson accepted the money.[17] Harold Seymour states that "Admitting that 'there is no disputing that some kind of plot existed,'...there is no 'incontrovertible' proof that the plot was carried out."[18] Edd Roush said, "I don't know whether the whole truth of what went on there among the White Sox will ever come out. Even today nobody really knows exactly what took place. The truth of the matter was inevitably left behind in the hotel rooms, bars, and pool halls that the implicated White Sox and their accomplices frequented.[19]

To further complicate the discovery of the truth, the news reporting of the day was inaccurate and biased, I dare say no different than today, but to a greater degree. Before the grand jury met, the reporters had feasted on interviews with a lot of the small time gamblers, especially, Bill Maharg, "Sleepy" Burns, and Abe Attel who seemed to be the crux of the gamblers involved in the "fix". The media had already made predictions and planted the seed that the players should be banished from the game. Is that what Judge Kenesaw Landis based his decision on?

There were conflicting reports. On September 29, 1921, Cicotte told the grand jury that he put nothing on the ball, and it was possible to count the seams, but on September 30, he said, "I pitched the best ball I knew how after that first ball. But I lost because I was hit, not because I was throwing the game." Is that first ball the one that was a strike or the one that hit Morrie Rath. Even accounts of the play by play differ from one report to another. Accounts of the game claim that the first pitch was a strike to Rath and not the bean ball that signaled that the "fix" was on.

Two reporters agreed that crime was "the most interesting of all news themes--judged by circulation gains and popular interest," and the Black Sox scandal was an exemplary crime. It had villains (the players and the gamblers; unsuspecting victims (Comiskey, young boys, and the nation); heroes (reporters, baseball officials, and players trying to clean up the game); a heinous crime (the manipulation of the national game); confessions (Eddie Cicotte, Joe Jackson, Lefty Williams, and Hap Felsch); and an uncertain conclusion.

The press rarely presumed the eight White Sox innocent, and likened the implicated players to Benedict Arnold and Judas Iscariot. "It was the exceptional newspaper that reported that "neither Jackson nor Williams had made any admission of 'game-throwing' to the grand jury, and that the fixers of the Series were unknown to them."[20] Very little was printed about that facts in the grand jury testimony. According to Asinof, neither baseball nor the media wanted to pursue an inquiry.[21] The press referred to the players as traitors, outlaws, snakes, and rats. The reporters who were against the players felt that the owners, public, and young boys had been swindled. Finally, the press made no effort to investigate the poor management-labor relationship of professional baseball nor the long standing association between professional baseball and gamblers--two of the main reasons for the "fix". Just before Kenesaw Mountain Landis became the Commissioner of baseball, Ban Johnson was pushing for legislation to make gambling on baseball a felony. Edd Roush of the Cincinnati Reds suggested that the media latched on to the story of a "fix" because it would explain why the team the press picked to win the World Series had done so poorly against the Reds.

One thing that is relatively certain is that the press knew about the "fix" before or early in the Series as exemplified by Christy Mathewson and Hugh Fullerton watching for signs of the White Sox throwing the series at the start of game 1. Ring Lardner and Jimmy Crusinberry, but not Hugh Fullerton, Comiskey's friend, at the request of the Sox manager, Kid Gleason, stood close to Gleason and Abe Attel in a bar and listened to Attel spill the beans. After game 2, Gleason also told Crusinberry about the telegrams Gleason received about the "fix." Crusinberry was silenced by his editor, mostly for fear of a libel suit.

The owners and the baseball establishment were not the "unsuspecting victims." The expected winners' share of the 1919 World Series was $2,000, and the expected losers' share was $1,400 which turned into $890 and $535 per player after war taxes and other deductions were figured in. Many letters to the editor of the *Chicago Tribune* held that the players were no more guilty than those who employed them. In March 1921, a letter to the *Chicago Herald and Examiner* stated: "If they are guilty, punish them all, but don't forget to punish also the higher ups; but if they are innocent, let the world know it just as when their suspected guilt was first discovered." "Fullerton noted that the 'public has for years had little faith and much disgust in the officials and club owners of the major league clubs. Rather than lend credence to the allegations of malfeasance on the part of the ballplayers, Fullerton argued that the 'fault for this condition lies primarily with the owners. Their commercialism is directly responsible for the same spirit among the athletes and their failure to punish even the appearance of evil has led to the present situation...'"[22] "Baseball owners were not about to air their dirty linen (or sox, in this case), not if they did not have to, and no one was making them."[23] Gene Carney makes the point that by "failing to give consideration to the different degrees of participation in the fix, and by pretending that banning eight players solved the problem, baseball officialdom has perpetuated cover-up." The 1919 World Series is one of baseball's Watergates. How many more are there? Would steroid abuse be rampant if it had not been bought to light?

William Cook and others make a strong case for Cincinnati beating the Sox outright; the Reds just outplayed the Sox. "Superb team work and effort had overcome the odds."[24] The Reds led the league in fielding average, fewest errors, and triples. "Every man focused on one goal-get the runner home."[25] And that is what the Reds did in the 1919 World Series, and that is what the White Sox failed to do. The Cincinnati Red Sox beat the New York Giants by nine games to win the pennant, but some thought that the Giants threw the season to the Reds. It was rumored that two Giant players, first baseman Hal Chase and third baseman Heinie Zimmerman were making errors on purpose. In the 1917 World Series against the White Sox, Zimmerman was involved in a botched run down in the fourth inning of one game with the score tied 0-0. In 1918, Zimmerman offered a teammate, pitcher Rube Benton, $800 to throw a game.[26] Zimmerman and Chase were banned from baseball for life in 1918, but Chase was exonerated in 1919. The White Sox had three starting pitchers at their disposal with concern about Cicotte's arm while the Reds had six starters available, and the Red's staff had a better ERA than the White Sox. The Reds were the first team in history to start five pitchers in a World Series. Cicotte pitched in 25 percent of the White Sox games in 1919, and his performance in the final games of the season was not impressive. The Reds had the second best batting average in the National League. Christy Mathewson and Hugh Fullerton, the reporters who looked for obvious bad plays during the

Series, could only identify seven questionable plays which Fullerton said "might equally have been caused by the accidents of the game."[27] Mathewson once wrote five arguments demonstrating how ridiculous he thought it was to question the honesty of the Series.[28] "Fullerton wrote, '…an evil minded person might believe the stories that have been circulated during the series. The fact is that this series was lost in the first game, and lost through overconfidence.'"[29] Ray Schalk, the White Sox catcher, said, to support Cook's thesis, "If Red [Urban Clarence] Faber, [the other Sox pitcher who missed the Series because of a sore ankle] had been able to pitch, I'm sure there would have been no Black Sox scandal." Finally, the White Sox were filled with egos and conflict with each other and with Comiskey while the Reds got along with each other and played as a team.

Supposedly, before game one, someone stopped Cicotte on the street and told him a man with a rifle was looking for him. In game 1, in the fourth inning, a bad relay from Swede Risberg to Chick Gandil failed to complete a double play that would have taken the Reds out of the inning without any runs, but it was in the fourth that the Reds put the game away by scoring five runs. The White Sox only had six hits and one run. Even if Cicotte were throwing the game, Cincinnati would have won. The White Sox played poorly except for George "Buck" Weaver (hit .324), Dick Kerr (2-0 with a 1.42 ERA), and Joe Jackson. After game one, the odds went from 8 to 5 on the White Sox to 7 to 10, but once again there is a discrepancy because Frommer claims that the odds were even money before game one. After game 2, the Reds were a 9 to 5 favorite.

There is more conflict; many historians feel that the White Sox turned on the gamblers after game two and played to win. Even the gamblers said that. "…in Harry Grabiner's diary, he recounts the story of the fix that the Sox obtained from gambler Harry Redmon, in which he said that Cicotte and Weaver were "crooked" in the first game and then turned."[30] "Hugh Fullerton wrote later the he had heard a story after Game Three about a meeting of players and gamblers that morning. Williams and Cicotte refused to go any further with it and…"[31] In a grand jury statement, Lefty Williams said that he spoke with Cicotte…after [game five]. "I told him we were double-crossed and that I was going to win if there was any possible chance. Cicotte said he was the same way."

Eliot Asinof's *Eight Men Out*, and its screen adaptation aspires to tell a more-or-less "true" story about the past.[32] Asinof is not an academic and so is not bound by the strictures of a professional discipline.[33] His book lacks verifiability which Asinof could have avoided if he used footnotes and included a bibliography. It conforms to numerous (but...not all) traditional historiographic conventions and thus satisfies the expectations of most readers of history. It is "most opaque and alien" in its treatment of facts.[34] As you will see later in the chapter entitled "Shoeless Joe", there are blatant historical errors. "Asinof wrote his version of things without ever seeing the grand jury statements, stolen before the "Black Sox trial" in 1921."[35] The historical value aside, Asinof concluded that Joe was more a victim than anything else.

And what has the commissioner's office done since the 1919 "Fix"? Justice from the commissioner's office has not been consistent, to say the least, before or after the 1919 Series. Hal Chase was exonerated by John Heydler in 1919 for throwing games over the course of two seasons against testimony by a number of players and managers. Why didn't Landis ban Chase from baseball. Chase is also implicated in arranging the "fix" of 1919. Heydler let Chase off because of a "lack of evidence," but the real reason was most likely to avoid a law suit. Heydler later said that "...his only regret in his career was 'not giving credence to Christy Mathewson in the Hal Chase case.' Had he done so, the scandal may never have occurred... He would be instrumental in the corruption of some of his former teammates on the White Sox."[36] Bowie Kuhn suspended Denny McLain for three months and put him on probation for alleged bookmaking. Granted, McLain was never accused officially of throwing a game.[37] Bud Selig notes: "In Shoeless Joe's case, there's so much history that needs to be looked at, and that's what we're trying to do, to understand why Judge Landis did what he did. He (Shoeless Joe) deserves a look."[38] In 1960, Commissioner Ford Frick turned down a request from David Susskind to present a drama involving the 1919 Black Sox scandal, and two months later he was criticized by *The Sporting News*. Frick was called a czar and his decision arbitrary. *The Sporting News* said, "To the best of anyone's knowledge, Jackson took no part in the fix..."[39] Peter Ueberroth confronted Pete Rose about Rose's gambling, and according to John Helyar, baseball "closed its eyes." General managers "wouldn't mess with a gold-plated attraction." Commissioner...Ueberroth..."did his part to cover up." Happy Chandler, who succeeded Judge Landis, was interviewed after he left office and said, "I don't think [Jackson] ever did anything in connection with that scandal. It is an injustice that ought to be corrected by baseball people."[40] What are they waiting for? This is a commissioner that was alive and witnessed that era of baseball. Commissioner Vincent stated that "we cannot go back in time...that he is reluctant to play God with history. Commissioner Landis certainly had no such qualms about playing God, not only with history, but with the lives of real people--people who had the misfortune of turning up in his courtrooms, especially his last one, his czardom, baseball."[41] But Vincent erased the asterisk beside Roger Maris' sixty-one home run record, overturning Ford Frick's 1961 ruling.

I would like to mention in passing, and I leave it to someone else to try to clear Buck Weaver, but he may have been judged wrongly, too. Abe Attel maintained that Weaver was guiltless and claimed to have tried to clear Weaver with Landis. Weaver did not go to management because he was sworn to secrecy by Chick Gandil and Swede Risberg, who threatened him with physical violence. Attel testified that Gandil told him that he could not get to Weaver. Maybe Baseball will reconsider both "Shoeless" Joe *and* Buck someday. Coincidentally, both Jackson and Weaver sued the White Sox for back pay and won.

CHAPTER 2

"Shoeless Joe"

Joseph Jefferson Jackson was not educated and even struggled in big, northern cities where baseball ruled as the national past time. He was semiliterate and very gullible. To his family, he was shy, unassuming, and considerate. To many others, he was a naïve busher, a fool, a dupe, a pathetic simpleton. Daniel Okrent says, "Had he (Joe Jackson) any sense of the consequences, there is no way he would have taken part in it (the "Fix"). But I don't think anyone could guess that a man as basically simple as Jackson could have known, really, what it meant what he was doing."[42] Furman Bisher, after a 1951 interview with Joe, concluded that Jackson was "a plain and simple man, who thought in plain and simple ways."[43]

Admittedly, there is a great deal of mystery surrounding the 1919 World Series, and the most controversial figure is Joseph Jefferson Jackson, "Shoeless Joe." Although he told the Grand Jury that he was a part of the "fixing" of the World Series, the reason he confessed is debated. Those who want to believe that his testimony was the truth will bunch him with the other seven conspirators, all of whom recanted their testimony, and some of whom claimed to be innocent. How Joe got involved is unknown also, because he was apparently not in the room the night before game 1 of the World Series. Supposedly, Lefty Williams drew him into the plot, and Joe requested $20,000 to join. When Lefty got $10,000 he gave Jackson $5,000. Another story has Chick Gandil approaching Joe in Boston and offering Jackson $10,000 to join the other seven in the "fix". Joe refused twice. A few days later, Gandil offered Joe $20,000, and Jackson refused again.

According to Joe, he was called into Charles (Commie) Comiskey's office and was told by Comiskey and Alfred Austrian, Comiskey's attorney, that he should confess to conspiring to throw the World Series, and Austrian would protect him; the grand jury was after the gamblers. Gene Carney concludes, "We do know that [Alfred Austrian, Charles Comiskey's attorney] made sure that Jackson waived his immunity [to the Grand Jury], something a lawyer acting on behalf of Jackson probably would not have advised."[44] He also offers that the reason was to silence Jackson and to continue the cover-up. Cicotte, Williams, and Jackson testified at the 1921 trial that they had not signed away their immunity. Jackson may have been duped by Austrian who told Jackson that Cicotte and Williams already signed statements incriminating Joe. On the witness stand, Jackson recalled Austrian telling him that he needed a lawyer "damn bad" because Jackson would be indicted shortly, and Austrian "promised if I'd tell what I knew I would not be prosecuted."[45] Joe signed a piece of paper that he couldn't read…a waiver of immunity. There is even a suggestion that Judge Charles A. McDonald, the chief justice of the Chicago grand jury, may have been in on getting Jackson to sign the waiver. William R. Herzog II, in his essay *The Faith of Fifty Million*, details better than most books the case for a connection between the cover-up of the fix and Jackson's banishment.[46] "Chicago lawyer David Carlson:

> It's my theory that [Alfred] Austrian and Comiskey wanted Jackson to confess so they could compromise him. Jackson was in the unique position of substantially embarrassing Comiskey by telling of his attempts to inform him of the fix."[47]

In the winter of 1919-20, "Shoeless" Joe with the help of his wife wrote a series of letters to Comiskey. On 19 November, Comiskey offered to "gladly pay your expenses to Chicago" if Jackson wanted to go there and tell what he knew about the Series. On November 15, Jackson wrote that he had been surprised to hear his name linked to the rumors of the fix, and he offered to go to Chicago any time. Twice in his letter, Jackson insisted that he had done all he could to win the Series. There was no reply. Conspiracy theorists might conclude that this is the evidence that Comiskey did not want Jackson's story on record. [Comiskey's] investigator was not directed to visit [Joe in] Savannah."[48]

Jackson and two other White Sox, Eddie Cicotte and Lefty Williams,--compelled by Comiskey, Austrian, and the state's attorney-- signed a confession and an agreement of immunity from prosecution without the benefit of legal counsel, but the agreements of immunity were actually waivers of immunity. The confessions and waivers of immunity were subsequently lost along with all of the evidence of the first Grand Jury hearing, but later surfaced in Comiskey's custody. I will discuss this in more detail in the *Comiskey* chapter. Supposedly, Williams named Cicotte, Gandil, Weaver, and Felsch and several gamblers, but not Joe. Joe may have been brought into the fray because he knew too much and would have implicated Comiskey in trying to cover everything up.

Prior to the Series, it is believed that Jackson approached Comiskey the day before the first game and asked not to play because he heard rumors of some players plotting to throw the Series. "It has been stated that Hugh Fullerton, a New York sports writer, was in Comiskey's room during Jackson's visit and heard the entire exchange."[49] Joe said, "I never said anything about it until the night before the Series started. I went to Mr. Comiskey and begged him to take me out of the lineup...If there was something going on I knew the bench would be the safest place, but he wouldn't listen to me."[50] Jackson supposedly tried to fake an illness to keep from playing in the first game of the Series, but Gleason, the White Sox manager, and Comiskey ordered Jackson to play. Why would someone who was in on the "fix" bring attention to himself? Joe also stated that he went to Comiskey "three weeks" before the Series.[51] Jackson was afraid because he claims that Swede Risberg, a teammate, threatened his life if he squealed. Joe also feared the mob. If his name was included with those throwing the Series, and the mob found out that he was not in on the fix, he feared there would be retribution. In fact, for these two reasons, he was given protective custody after his testimony to the Grand Jury.

One fact that is continuously mentioned to support the fact the Shoeless Joe did not partake in the conspiracy is his statistics. He hit .375, leading both teams, with 6 of the 17 White Sox RBIs which was third behind Duncan (8 of 33) and Roush (7 of 33) of the Reds; had a World Series record 12 hits; had a .563 slugging percentage; threw out one player at the plate and may have thrown out another, but the catcher bobbled the ball; and Cicotte deflected another which may have been an out. Joe hit the only home run of the Series and committed no errors in thirty attempts (fielding and/or throwing of the sixteen balls he made plays on). This was better than he played in the 1917 World Series when he hit .304 with 2 RBIs, and the White Sox *won* that World Series.

Joe wanted to win the 1919 World Series. He would sit in a dark room with a candle and stare at the flame; he claimed this strengthened his vision and improved his concentration. He collected hair pins as a good luck charm. He intensified his fetish for the hair pins and spent more time staring at the candle preparing for the 1919 World Series.

The counter argument against Jackson's 1919 World Series statistics points out that he did not get many of his hits in critical situations, and the home run came when the game was out of reach and of no consequence. Assuming the "fix" was off after game 5, in the first five games Jackson came to bat with eleven men on base and never drove in a run, but after game 5 he drove in six runs. But if you compare two players from that same game who are in the Hall of Fame, Eddie Collins and Edd Roush, they did no better. In game four (Cincinnati 2- Chicago 0), Jackson made a throw to the plate that most observers feel would have cut the runner down if it had not been cut off. In game six, Jackson threw out Larry Rath at home trying to score on a sacrifice fly which ended the fourth inning with Cincinnati leading 4-0. The White Sox fought back and won the game in 10 innings, 5-4. In game seven (Chicago 4- Cincinnati 1), pitched by Cicotte, Jackson drove in 2 of the 4 White Sox runs. Cook concludes that "…when one examines separately the level of involvement for each one of the eight White Sox players that were indicted by the grand jury away from the collective core of the less than ten suspicious plays, their individual involvement appears to be more passive than blatantly corrupt."[52] Also, although Jackson was 0 for 4 in game one, he advanced two runners which was more than his teammates combined. In the deadball era, advancing runners was a must. Joe hit to the right side to advance runners in games one, four, and seven. In game two, he went 3 for 4. Skeptics say that Joe was just "poking" at the ball, but the facts are that he hit a Texas leaguer that he hustled into a double, a single behind Weaver, and a hard smash that the first baseman knocked down but threw too late to get Jackson. There were also a number of great defense plays by both teams. When the White Sox were leading or trailing by three or less runs, Jackson hit .435 (10 for 23). He hit well against a pitching staff that was better than the White Sox's staff, he hit safely in six of eight games with five multi-hit games, and struck out twice in 32 at bats. "To suggest that he intentionally hit better in certain games than in others is to suggest that he could rack up hits at will, whenever he wanted, which is ridiculous."[53]

One piece of evidence that is glossed over is *sabermetrics*. In 1984, Bennett and Flueck used data from two baseball seasons to estimate the probability the home team wins a game given the run differential (the home team runs minus visiting team runs), the half inning (top or bottom of the inning), the number of outs, and the on-base situation. Using these estimated probabilities, one can see how the probability of winning changes for each game event. One can measure a player's contribution to winning a game by summing the changes in win probabilities for each play in which the player has participated. This statistic, called the Player Game Percentage, was used by Bennett (1993) to evaluate the batting performance of Joe Jackson. This player was banished from baseball for allegedly throwing the 1919 World Series. A statistical analysis using the Player Game Percentage showed that Jackson played to his full potential during this series.[54]

Joe was not a well educated person, and for him to plan so well as to choose when to play well and when his play would be inconsequential seems a bit far fetched. Whichever is the truth, he certainly did not make it look as obvious as some of the others in the conspiracy that he was throwing the series. He even testified before the Grand Jury that he batted, ran the bases, and fielded to win and did nothing to throw any game in the World Series. He played better in the 1919 World Series than he did in the 1917 World Series that the White Sox won. In an interview in 1950, just before he died, Shoeless Joe said, "I played my heart out in that series." "Although there was no Most Valuable Player award in 1919, years later baseball expert Bill Deane published his "What If" awards and chose Edd [Roush] as MVP of the National League and Joe Jackson MVP of the American League."[55]

Although Jackson was not educated, he had a lot of business smarts and common sense. He had a mini-conglomerate in the entertainment business with his "Baseball Girls." He also was part owner in a pool hall and farm.

Ed Bang, a member of the press corps covering the 1919 Series said that Ed Strong named eight players and concluded with "and they are taking poor Joe Jackson for a ride."

Eight Men Out, the book published in 1963 and the movie, are the most cited documentaries supporting the events of the 1919 World Series. The book is not a history book, and the film is not a documentary. First, some of the portrayals in *Eight Men Out* are proven false. The stale champagne in the dugout after the White Sox clinched the pennant occurred after the 1917 season. Asinof makes it look like the White Sox were a shoe-in to win the World Series, but Cook points out that the teams were close on paper, and both had very strong pitching and could score runs. The Reds team ERA was 2.23 with 89 complete games and 23 shutouts versus the White Sox ERA of 3.04 with 88 complete games and 14 shutouts. Cincinnati had a better fielding percentage and had fewer fielding errors than the White Sox (152 vs. 176). According to Cook, contrary to Asinof's portrayal, Shoeless Joe did not sit on the bench feigning illness to convince Kid Gleason to keep him out of the game. Asinof portrayed the first pitch of Game 1 as a hit batsman, and that signaled that the "fix" was on. In reality, Cicotte's first pitch to Cincinnati's lead off batter, Morrie Rath, was a strike. Also, there is no evidence to support the death threat to Lefty William's wife, aside from an interview with his wife in 1959, as portrayed by Asinof. Second, Eliot Asinof has no documented support for the account. *Eight Men Out* is not an academic, historical report of the 1919 World Series; it is a story about the 1919 World Series based, in part, on facts with some literary fiction.

Eight Men Out portrays Joe taking an envelope containing part of Jackson's share of the payoff. Other accounts claim that the envelope was thrown on Jackson's bed, and he tried to give the money to Comiskey. Other accounts do not know what happened to the money or if Jackson got any money at all. Joe did testify to the Grand Jury that he received $5,000 and was promised $20,000 by Gandil, which is most likely true from various accounts, but Joe said that he played to win and did not try to throw any of the games. Whether this testimony was part of the confession that Comiskey had Joe sign, and Joe was playing along under the assumption that Comiskey and Austrian would protect him is not certain. After the state prosecutor stated that the confessions and immunity waivers had been lost, Jackson retracted this testimony and claimed that he did not partake in the "fix". As a matter of fact, he always contended that he played to the best of his ability which is one thing that he never changed. There are other facts that did change over the years as you will see in the next paragraph. The Grand Jury exonerated Jackson and the other seven; I will return to this in the *Landis* chapter.

The pay off is even controversial. What is certain is that Joe did get $5,000. According to Jackson, after the last game, Lefty Williams went into Jackson's room with two dirty envelopes in his hand and told Joe, "One of these is for you, Joe. Jackson also said that it was after game 4. Some of the players sold the Series to a gambling clique. We told that clique that you would play crooked ball, too. There's $5,000 in the envelope. It's not all what we were promised, but it's better than getting nothing." Jackson told Williams that Joe did not want the money and that Lefty "had a hell of a lot of nerve using my name in the affair." Williams testified that he had used Jackson's name without Joe's knowledge and that Jackson "played his regular game all the way through."[56] Next was when Joe went to Comiskey. Jackson was dismissed by Harry Grabiner, the general manager and secretary to Comiskey. Grabiner told Joe, "We know what you want." He showed the money to Grabiner and asked him what to do with it. Grabiner told him "to take the money and go" home to Savanah. "[T]he cash that might have made Joe Jackson a hero for blowing the whistle on the fix instead condemned him when he could not prove that he had showed it to his employer."[57] That Joe took the money is certain because he and Katie Jackson, believing that the money was not theirs, put it in a savings account and let it earn interest. After Katie's death, "the money…was donated to the American Heart Fund and the American Cancer Society." Finally, there is no evidence of Joe ever being in the room where the ball players gathered to discuss the "fix."

On September 23, 1920, New York Giants pitcher, Rube Benton, testified at a grand jury probe that a Cincinnati betting commissioner named Hahn told him that five White Sox players demanded $100,000 to throw the series, and that was paid to them by a group of Pittsburgh gamblers. Benton specifically named Ed Cicotte, Claude Williams, Chick Gandill, and Happy Felsch. He did not remember the fifth man's name, but Buck Weaver, Joe Jackson, Eddie Collins, John (Shano) Collins, and Ray Schalk were not mentioned by Hahn.[58] Hahn could never be found, and Benton's testimony could have been false since two unnamed Cubs players testified to the grand jury that Benton bragged about winning $8,000. A man by the name of Hahn, located in Pittsburgh, was implicated as the brains behind the "fix," and Abe Attell was his right-hand man.

"Despite the confessions, it was unclear who did not play to the best of his ability during the series, who had accepted money from gamblers, who knew what and when."[59]

In 1924, Joe won a law suit against Comiskey for back wages from the World Series, $16,700, but received no settlement because Judge John J. Gregory said that Jackson committed perjury in his statement to the Cook County grand jury. Gregory ruled that his opinion outweighed that of the jury.[60] Irving Vaughn wrote, "in plain every-day language, the jury found that the White Sox officials perpetrated a fraud when Jackson was signed and that they had knowledge of the crooked work in the series at that time." Ray Cannon, Joe's lawyer, said, "We view the victory obtained by Jackson from a jury of twelve men and women to be so far reaching as to bring about Jackson's ultimate return to organized baseball." In that trial, Comiskey testified under oath that he believed that Joe played to the best of his ability even though Comiskey stood to lose $16,000 if he lost the law suit. The jury was asked to decide whether Jackson "did lawfully conspire with Gandill, Williams, and other members of the White Sox Club, or any of them, to lose or 'throw' any of the baseball games of the 1919 World Series to the Cincinnati Baseball Club?", and eleven of twelve answered, "No." "In their special verdict by eleven to one, [the jury found] that the money had been given *after*, not during the Series, and that Williams did *not* tell Jackson at that time that the cash was his share of the money received for the players' part in an agreement with gamblers to toss the Series."[61]

In 1951, Joseph Jefferson Jackson was inducted as a charter member of the Cleveland Indians Baseball Hall of Fame. Many in Cleveland believed that Jackson was the victim of a bum rap, exploited by Comiskey, ensnared by (Jewish) city slickers, and punished extralegally by Landis. In 1993, San Francisco's Court of Historical

Review ruled that Joe Jackson ought to be reinstated by Major League Baseball.

John Lardner in "Remember the Black Sox" concluded that some of [the banished ballplayers], fix or no fix, were never paid money to throw a game.[62] To his death, Shoeless Joe Jackson swore he did not partake in the throwing of the 1919 World Series.

Ray Schalk who suspected crooked play during the Series said that Joe Jackson played the Series to win. In 1999, Ted Williams said that Eddie Collins, who was a member of the Red Sox executive staff when Ted played for the Boston Red Sox, told him that Joe Jackson was not in on the "fix" of the 1919 World Series. Ted Williams, along with Bob Feller and Hank Aaron have been soliciting support to have Shoeless Joe cleared in the "fix" and have Jackson admitted to the Baseball Hall of Fame.

Chick Gandil said that he and his teammates conspired to fix the World Series, but, in the end, they double-crossed the gamblers and played to win and losing "was pure baseball fortune." In 1920 Jackson told the Grand Jury that "[Chick Gandil] asked me to consider $10,000 to frame something up and I asked him frame what? And he told me and I said no. [Gandil] just walked away from me, and when I returned to Chicago, he told me that he would give me twenty and I said no again, and on the bridge where you go into the club house he told me I could either take it or let it alone, they were going through. They said, "You might as well say yes or say no and play ball or anything you want…[S]ome of the gamblers who testified that Joe Jackson was in on the fix…[said] [t]hey had been told he was by Chick Gandil."[63] In 1924, Lefty Williams testified that he used Jackson's name in the meetings with gamblers without Jackson's knowledge or permission and that Joe was not in on the "fix." Did Joseph Jefferson Jackson, a poor, uneducated kid from South Carolina, but with a lot of business sense, dupe the gamblers? In an editorial that appeared on February 14, 1924, as the Jackson v. Comiskey trial ended, *The Sporting News* wrote, "…while he did take part of the gambler's money, he only double-crossed them and was not a party to the actual selling of the Series."[64] Was his name used by the other crooked White Sox? In a 1951 *Atlantic Journal-Constitution* article, Thurman Bisher concluded that [Jackson's] weakness…had been that [Joe] relied too heavily on his friends for guidance; in 1919 he had put his trust in bad hands, [and he] did not realize he was doing anything wrong."[65] Most historians believe that "Shoeless" Joe played to win. Contemporary historians more than writers who lived decades later felt that Joe did nothing wrong. Who is more believable, those who lived in Joe's era or those leafing through mounds of manuscripts in search of evidence, and sometimes evidence used only to support their contentions? Ray Schalk, the White Sox catcher, felt that Cicotte and Jackson gave their best.

The consensus of opinion of historians is that Jackson went to Comiskey early in the Series if not before. Comiskey and Alfred Austrian and maybe Judge McDonald conspired to get Joe to sign a false confession and a waiver of immunity, and "Shoeless" Joe became a scapegoat to save Comiskey. Jackson made Comiskey aware that "the ways and means to throwing games [were] discussed," did not "entertain proposal[s] of promises to throw a game, [or] sit in conference with a bunch of crooked players and gamblers."

Joe Jackson recorded the third best all-time career batting average behind Ty Cobb, the same person who admitted to betting on baseball, and Rogers Hornsby. Is *the wrong man out* and are *the wrong men in*?

CHAPTER 3

Comiskey

Charles Albert Comiskey is far from an innocent victim of the 1919 Chicago White Sox alleged "fixing" of the World Series. It is an accepted fact that Comisky paid his players less than their worth in 1919. Player for player, the White Sox were paid less than comparable players of that era. That is one of the reasons given for the players conspiring to lose the World Series. Comiskey supposedly kept Cicotte on the bench at the end of the 1919 season because Cicotte had an incentive provision in his contract paying him a bonus if he won 30 games. With one week left in the season, Comiskey ordered Kid Gleason, the manager, to hold Cicotte out for the rest of the season, however there is no evidence to support this. William Cook argues that the the White Sox pitching staff was injured, and Cicotte was held out to rest him for the World Series. "George Cicotte, a great grandnephew of Eddie Cicotte, has claimed that...the scene in the movie *Eight Men Out* depicting Comiskey denying Cicotte a bonus was "highly accurate.""[66] He also substantiates that Eddie's wife was threatened during the 1919 World Series which Cicotte claimed to be the reason that he pitched poorly in his last game of the Series.

Comiskey was a powerful, upright man, a baseball pioneer, but his best friends could not call him a lavish spender--not with the hired help. Comiskey's pay scale for his players was lower than most, and his players were better than any. During the 1919 season, he was locked in a bitter salary dispute with the players over being underpaid compared to the rest of Major League baseball. Ty Cobb was making $20,000 a year and Joe Jackson was making $6,000. At one point the team asked Kid Gleason, the manager, to intervene on their part, but he came back empty handed which further embittered the players. Oddly, in 1915, Cleveland traded Joe Jackson to the White Sox for an outfielder, pitcher, and $31,500. It was one of the highest cash transactions to that time for a major league player. Comiskey claimed that he was paying Jackson $10,000 a year when he was only paying him $6,000. There was no free agency in 1919, and the White Sox salaries were determined by Comiskey without discussion or appeal. When it came time to pay the players their share of the World Series money ($1,952.75), he gave them $1,500.00. Researcher Bob Hoie argues that the 1919 White Sox had the top payroll in their league and perhaps in both leagues.

While other teams were paying players four dollars a day for meals, Comiskey paid his players three dollars a day. He also charged his players fifty cents to clean their uniforms. Meanwhile, Comiskey was wining and dining his friends at his lodge and in the clubhouse under his players' noses. Comiskey had lavish parties and hunting trips for the press and his friends; he served them champagne at press conferences in the locker room while his players got flat, less than tasty champagne after winning the 1917 pennant. This was "the bonus that Comiskey promised the players for winning the flag." Ring Lardner said, "It tasted like stale piss." In this day and age, Comiskey may be considered a co-conspirator. Nonetheless, he certainly wasn't the poor, innocent victim.

He always treated the press well, and the press never painted Comiskey as a self-important, manipulative, ruthless man. Therefore, baseball fans never saw that side of Comiskey.

There is a reasonable amount of evidence that Comiskey got wind of a conspiracy before the Series concluded and made no honest effort to investigate; Jackson may have told Comiskey point blank. Comiskey may have known even before the Series started. Joe Jackson claims to have told him so. Hugh Fullerton, loyal to Comiskey to the end, after Comiskey's death wrote in *The Sporting News* that Fullerton had informed the baseball authorities, including Charles Comiskey, before game one that the "fix" was in.

Comiskey claims to have investigated the issue, but found no good evidence. He said that there were rumors and "yarns spun out of the bitterness over losing wager."[67] He offered a reward for "information confirming team members' crookedness. Although he was apparently presented with information indicating that the rumors had some factual basis, Comiskey--advised by his friend Alfred Austrian, a prominent Chicago attorney--chose to do nothing."[68] Harry Grabiner's, Comiskey's secretary, diary reveals, "beyond any doubt, that the White Sox front office had more than some inkling what was going on from the very first game of the 1919 World Series."[69] Grabiner states in his diary that after the first game when Mont Tennes, a noted Chicago gambler and friend of Comiskey, called Grabiner, and intimated that there was something wrong with the Series. After game one, Kid Gleason received telegrams from concerned White Sox fans, and Tennes informed Gleason that there were rumors of a "fix". Later that night, Gleason met with Comiskey and showed him the telegrams. Comiskey then met with John Hydler, the National League President, and passed the information to him. They both then went to Byron Bancroft "Ban" Johnson, the American League President with whom Comiskey was not on speaking terms because of a misunderstanding involving trout that Comiskey sent Johnson that arrived stale and smelly, and told Johnson. Johnson said, "What he [Comiskey] says is like the crying of a whipped cur." Only after the story hit the press did Comiskey suspend the eight ball players. If he knew about the Fix after Game Two why didn't he suspend the players then? He supposedly concealed the "fix" for the sake of success on the field and at the gates. Harry Grabiner stated in his diary that Comiskey went to Heydler after the White Sox returned to Chicago which would have been after Game Two. Supposedly, Hydler made the statement that "there are rumors of fixes every year."[70] No matter what, Gene Carney concludes that "From the day Comiskey was convinced that some of his players were lying down in the Series-and this was very early, because the first two games confirmed all the rumors he had heard-he seemed to be doing his best to simultaneously collect all the evidence he could and suppress that evidence…But it seems clear that Comiskey had enough evidence right after the Series to act. And he did: he withheld the Series checks of the eight players whom he had heard-from gamblers and reporters, and probably Gleason and Schalk-were involved."[71]

After the 1919 Series ended, Ray Schalk, one of the White Sox, issued some strong statements and echoed what the writer, Hugh Fullerton, had said that seven of the White Sox would not return, but prior to the 1920 season, probably under pressure from Comiskey, Schalk retracted his statement and said, "I played to the best of my ability. I feel that every man on our club did the same, and there was not a single moment of all the games in which we did not try." Then, Comiskey went on to sign Cicotte with a $5,000 increase in salary,

Williams with a $3,000 increase, and Felsch with a $3,000 increase. Joe Jackson held out signing his contract until Grabiner went to Savannah and pressured Joe into signing a three year contract for $8,000 a year. Grabiner said, "We've got the goods on Cicotte, Williams, and Gandil. We know who was guilty in throwing the Series. We know it all and how much each man got in being crooked. We know you discussed fixing the World Series with Gandil and that Williams gave you $5,000....Cicotte and Williams wrongfully used your name...You can take what I'm offering, or you can leave it. You well know that we can do anything we want with you, with any of you. You take it, or we kick you out of baseball." So without the help of Katie, Joe's wife, to read the contract to him, Joe signed that contract. These raises may have merely reflected the improved financial condition of baseball since the entire team received raises of approximately 32 percent.

Later, Comiskey stated, "There is always some scandal of some kind following a big sporting event like the World Series. These yarns are manufactured out of whole cloth and grow out of bitterness due to losing wagers. I believe my boys fought the battles of the recent World Series on the level, as they have always done."

Although Comiskey offered a $10,000 reward for information proving that White Sox players threw the 1919 World Series, he never paid that out. In the Jackson v. Comiskey trial, it came out that the letter from his investigators on May 11, 1920 was virtually empty and with it was a bill for $3,820.71 and not the $10,000 Comiskey claimed to have spent to find the truth. Most authors feel the investigation was simply a show by Comiskey. He discarded the testimony of the gamblers concluding that small-time gamblers could not fix the World Series. His "first impulse was to hush it up; 'only later would he adopt the role of outraged defender of baseball's purity'"[72] "...the magnates were our best friends for a while. They wanted to hush it up... The magnates were in cahoots with the lawyers."[73]

"Comiskey and his lawyers received most of the names of the St. Louis gamblers...early in their investigation. This may have come from the owner of the Cincinnati Reds, Garry Herrmann. They chose to ignore what Ban [Johnson]...chose to pursue."[74] All through Johnson's tenure as commissioner, there are repeated references to the need for "crackdowns" on "gambling".[75] The consensus of opinion is that Comiskey ignored the information because he did not want to pay the $10,000 reward that he was offering for evidence that his players threw the World Series. Frank G. Menke of *The Sporting News*, after the 1924 Jackson v. Comiskey trial charged that one day after the Series, Jackson displayed the $5,000 to Grabiner. Two days later, Comiskey knew the identity of the seven White Sox players involved in the "Fix", and neither Grabiner or Comiskey made a determined effort to "ferret out the real secret of the World Series crookedness of 1919 and both of the officials permitted all of the crooked men to resume play in the White Sox lineup of 1920."[76] Comiskey admitted at the trial that he knew the identity of the crooked players two days after the Series but made no attempt to get signed statements from them. Comiskey kept it covered up because it would wreck his team.[77] Menke concluded after Comiskey's testimony in 1924 that "Comiskey had engineered a cover-up, and it nearly worked."[78] The cover-up was far better organized than the "fix."

"Ban Johnson's investigators "uncovered the real truth"-- they knew who the guilty players were, and when they told Johnson, he "immediately took it to the office of the D.A. and asked for indictments." It may be that Johnson wanted to ruin Comiskey and his White Sox. "In Grabiner's diary is the suggestion that Ban Johnson had been "waiting patiently" for Charles A. McDonald to be made chief justice in Chicago…to wreck Comiskey and the White Sox so that Johnson and "the conspiracy" (an organization)…could purchase the franchise."[79] The day that McDonald was sworn in as Chief Justice, he directed the grand jury to turn its attention to baseball, not the Fix, but the Cubs-Phillies game that was thought to be tainted.

Comiskey was feuding with Ban Johnson, the baseball commissioner at the time, and Comisky wanted Johnson out. Comiskey blamed Johnson for not following up on the rumors of a "fix" of the 1919 World Series. Comisky was also a friend of Judge Kenesaw Mountain Landis, and Comiskey was influential in getting Landis appointed commissioner after Johnson was removed. It was a race between Ban Johnson and Charles Comiskey because Johnson wanted Comiskey out of baseball and Judge McDonald installed as commissioner, and Comiskey wanted Landis to replace Johnson. I will discuss this in more detail in the *Landis* chapter. In the spring of 1924,

Frank Menke traced the "Lasker Plan" to dethrone [Ban] Johnson and install Landis [as the commissioner of baseball] to Pittsburgh owner Barney Dreyfuss and Alfred Austrian.[80] Baseball, at the time, was corrupt with gambling and betting on games by the players, and players actually throwing games on which they bet. Comiskey may have wanted to try to clean up baseball, to his praise, and that may be why he wanted Landis as the baseball commissioner.

Was Comiskey so dedicated to bringing honor to baseball that he would allow his team to lose the World Series and suffer the consequences? He said that he would fire anyone proven to conspire to throw the World Series, but, even after signed confessions to the Grand Jury, he did not fire anyone. Bill Veeck, Jr. asserts that "...everybody did the best to cover up. *Everybody.* From the Commissioner on down."[81] "The state's [Illinois] attorney in charge of the prosecution [for the "Fix"] advised that Comiskey should be indicted along with the players, [based] on certain evidence in his hands."[82] Ban Johnson stopped it. He would not hear of such a thing.[83]

Speaking of the signed confessions and the transcript of the testimony, four years after the eight baseball players were exonerated, the confessions and transcript mysteriously appeared in Mr. Austrian's brief case during the civil trial of Jackson v. Comiskey. Austrian testified in the suit that Joe Jackson brought against Comiskey for back wages, "We got the grand jury records from the state's attorney of Cook County after the [1921] trial."[84] After Rothstein testified to the grand jury, Ban Johnson pronounced him innocent, as did Alfred Austrian, and Rothstein and Comiskey became allies. Corruption was commonplace at that time, and it would not be far fetched to think that Comiskey, and probably Arnold Rothstein, had someone paid off to "lose" the evidence. William Fallon, Rothstein's lawyer, admitted having copies "forwarded by his Chicago legal representative, Henry J. Berger."[85]

Maybe Comiskey didn't think that Landis would ban the eight Chicago White Sox players from baseball, and the White Sox could make a run at the 1920 World Series. They were considered the best baseball team at the time, and the future looked good for the Sox. Remember, free agency was many years off, and the players were, in a sense, slaves of the baseball owners. Comiskey could have kept the

White Sox intact for a number of years; only a few of the players were nearing the end of their careers. But, this is speculation, and I would prefer to stick with the facts.

Charles Dryden of the *Chicago Herald and Examiner* stated about Comiskey, borrowing a story from the holy writ, "The serpent he had warmed up and fed for many years bit him twice." The "Black Sox" were "bitter men with a common enemy: Charles Albert Comiskey."[86] Asinoff contends that Comiskey and the other baseball magnates did their best to ensure that the conspiracy remained out of the public view.[87] David Voigt notes that Comiskey's "long delayed action revealed him a man who put personal profit ahead of integrity and who remained silent in the face of known corruption."[88]

Charles Comiskey is in the Baseball Hall of Fame, but Joseph Jefferson Jackson is not. Comiskey and his fellow team owners exploited the ballplayers and tolerated the conditions that caused game fixing.[89] Both Voigt and Seymour argue that many people besides the implicated ballplayers, most notably gamblers and Comiskey, were responsible for the 1919 World Series debacle.[90] In fact, the one unanimous conclusion reached by all of the historian authors is that Comiskey was as much to blame for the alleged "fix" as the ballplayers themselves. In March 1921, to reiterate from chapter one, "If they are guilty, punish them all, but don't forget to punish also the higher ups; but if they are innocent, let the world know it just as when their suspected guilt was first discovered." In the October 28, 2005 New York Times, Studs Terkel wrote, "If there had been real justice after the scandal of 1919, Charlie Comiskey, the Sox owner, would have been the one kicked out of the game."[91] Marvin Miller asked, "I've always maintained that the question "Why isn't Shoeless Joe in the Hall of Fame?" should be supplemented with "Why isn't Charles Comiskey out?"[92] To paraphrase Judge Landis, " [anyone] that [knows about] the ways and means to throwing games are discussed, and does not promptly tell his [superior] about it, will never [be a part of a] professional baseball team." I guess Landis' ruling only applied to players and no one else because he certainly did not mention owners, commissioner, or "anyone" else. Is *the wrong man out*, and is *the wrong man in*?

Chapter 4

"Landis"

Judge Kenesaw Mountain Landis had a reputation of ruling with an iron fist. He enjoyed the power of his position as a judge, and when asked to be the commissioner of baseball, he accepted under the condition that he answered to no one. Ban Johnson, the baseball commissioner prior to Landis, called Landis a "pompous fraud."

Landis was an unorthodox judge whose decisions were often reversed on appeal. He was an egoist and showman; he was short-tempered, mean-spirited, egomaniacal, and despotic. He was a "tobacco-chewing bourbon drinker who would hand out stiff sentences to people who violated Prohibition. He had a knack for self-dramatizing publicity. [He] tried to extradite Kaiser Wilhelm on murder charges because a Chicagoan died when a German submarine sank the *Lusitania*."[93]

Judge Landis may have been courting the job of commissioner as early as January 1915 when the Federal League brought an antitrust suit against Major League Baseball. Landis was known as a hardliner against trusts, but he procrastinated and court costs skyrocketed. By the end of the 1915 season, the Federal League was ready to collapse. As a result of his stalling tactics, he enhanced his image with the major league owners and put them in his debt. The *Sporting News* said, "He's the game's good friend."

The aura at the time was that baseball was a means to raising the American youth with integrity and a sense of fair play. Baseball was felt to be a tester of manhood, a valuable educational tool, and not just a game. Foreman of the "Black Sox" Grand Jury, Henry H. Brigham, asserted that "the grand jurors are fully agreed that baseball has been a constructive moral influence to American life. Every normal boy learns to play and to love baseball." Landis argued that "Honesty in baseball is necessary for the continuance as the great American game and it must be kept clean at all hazards. It was more than just a "great American game"; it was ingrained in the moral fabric of American youth. Landis said that "Baseball is something more than a game to an American boy; it is his training field for life. Destroy his faith in its squareness and honesty and you have destroyed something more; you have planted suspicion of all things in his heart." W.J. Macbeth of the *New York Tribune* wrote: "Presuming all [ballplayers] are acquitted it will give Judge K.M. Landis an opportunity to prove himself savior of baseball." This was only more the reason for Landis to ban the eight White Sox players--to feed his mean-spirited, egomaniacal, despotic personality which was contemptuous of the judicial system that he was a part of. As the game's leaders had hoped, Landis established himself as someone who would not tolerate dishonesty.

In March 1921 Landis expelled Gene Paulette, a utility player with the St. Louis Cardinals, for associating with gamblers. A month later, he placed Benny Kauff of the New York Giants on the ineligible list when he was charged with involvement in a stolen automobile syndicate. Kauff was found not guilty, but Landis refused to reinstate him. Ray Fisher of the 1919 Cincinnati Reds was asked to take a $1,000 cut in his salary after the 1920 season. Fisher requested his release from the Reds to accept an offer to become the baseball and freshman football coach at the University of Michigan, and Landis banned Fisher for life from major league baseball for requesting the release. In 1980, Commissioner Bowie Kuhn reinstated Fisher as a player in good standing with major league baseball. Scandals from the past kept popping up, to the dismay of Landis, who finally declared a kind of amnesty. I guess Landis got tired of cleaning up baseball instead of doing his job, which can be questioned as to how well he did it.

Landis was a White Sox fan and attended a number of the 1919 World Series games. He gave no indication during the Series that the games were fixed. After game 2 of the Series, Landis commented, "The Reds are the most formidable machine I have ever seen in my many years as a fan. Individually and collectively the team is wonderful. I have learned through years of experience on the bench to maintain a judicial attitude, and I promise to do this provided the Reds do not keep on making this such a lopsided affair." As a fan, but with the power given to him by the baseball club owners, what a great opportunity to pay back the players that allegedly caused his team to lose the World Series--ban them from baseball for life.

In March 1921, Landis placed the eight indicted players on the ineligible list; this was after Comiskey had already suspended them in September 1920. Was this a power play by Landis? Surely he must have known that Comiskey had suspended them. On August 4, 1921 Judge Landis banned the eight White Sox and Fred McMullin for life. Hal Chase, who was thought to be instrumental in the fix and McMullin were indicted and posted bond, and California refused to extradite them. Chase was not banned.

Landis' famous decision:

> "Regardless of the verdict of juries, no player that throws a ball game, no player that entertains proposal of promises to throw a game, no player that sits in conference with a bunch of crooked players and gamblers where the ways and means to throwing games are discussed, and does not promptly tell his club about it, will ever play professional baseball."

Hugh Fullerton claims that he heard Joe Jackson tell Comiskey that there was a fix. Was that not "promptly" enough for Landis? In *Burying the Black Sox*, Gene Carney concludes that "The 1921 trial was not about justice, it was about image." And Landis was to insure the good image of baseball.

Hal Chase aside, why didn't Landis ban Ty Cobb and Tris Speaker for life when Hubert "Dutch" Leonard charged them and Joe Wood of the Boston Red Sox with throwing games between Detroit and Cleveland in 1919? Risberg, one of the alleged ring leaders of the 1919 World Series "fix", had pooled $1,100 and paid the Detroit Tigers to throw two doubleheaders late in the season. Risberg told Landis. An investigation revealed that the Tigers did indeed get the money, but it was deemed a gift rather than a bribe. Landis said, "It was an act of impropriety, reprehensible and censurable, but not an act of criminality." Why would the White Sox pool their money to reward Detroit for a deed already done? It makes no sense. Cobb even admitted that he was involved in gambling, but he used the same defense that Pete Rose used later: he only bet on his team to win and never played to lose. So, Cobb sat "in conference with a bunch of crooked players and gamblers where the ways and means to throwing games are discussed, and [did] not promptly tell his club about it" and is still in the Hall of Fame.

And the White Sox were deemed innocent by a court of law, and, therefore, theirs was not an "act of criminality." With judicial experience, Landis should have been consistent in his punishment, but he was wrapped up in himself, his position, and his power. Landis initially used the 1919 scandal to establish his discretionary power and thereafter used memories of it to protect and solidify his position. In "Say It Ain't So, Joe!," Thompson and Boswell concede that documentation is slight and based almost entirely on circumstantial evidence. Even the "Clean Sox" knew that something was wrong, and more than once they admitted as such, but they did nothing about it.[94] Eddie Collins told Landis that Buck Weaver placed a $40 bet for Collins that the Sox would sweep Detroit on Labor Day 1917. Collins is in the Hall of Fame. There was no repercussion for betting on a game in which he was involved.

Were Landis and Comiskey conspiring to show the country that they were dead set on "cleaning up baseball?" Did Landis double cross Comiskey? "(David Q.) Voight contends that the baseball establishment, led by Judge Kenesaw Mountain Landis, had an obvious vested interest in promoting the Black Sox scandal as a singular transgression."[95] This would ignore what baseball and the owners were doing to the players while singling out eight baseball players. "Landis, by keeping the focus on a minimum number of players, was doing exactly what the owners (especially Comiskey, who had a large hand in hiring Landis) wanted. Baseball's image would suffer no more than it had already. Management's role, *baseball's* role in covering up the ties between the sport and gambling, was not to be explored, or even mentioned.[96] Bill Veeck, Jr. stated:

> Landis's great wisdom was in understanding that any attempt to investigate all of the gambling and fixing of the past would not only be impossible from a purely administrative standpoint, but would open a can of worms that would be eating away at baseball for the next decade."[97]

The focus was kept on the players and swept away from the owners and gambling. Nelson Algren called it "a legal mugging by an enraptured Puritan."[98]

What happened to "innocent until proven guilty"? A jury exonerated the White Sox players. Even if they were indicted, they are still presumed innocent. The implicated White Sox players were deemed innocent according to our laws but Landis made himself judge <u>and</u> jury. Landis declared, "Regardless of the verdict of juries, no player who throws a ball game, no player that undertakes or promises to throw a ball game, no player that sits in a conference with a bunch of crooked players and gamblers where the ways and means of throwing a game are discussed, and does not promptly tell his club about it will ever play professional baseball." Had Landis already made up his mind well before becoming commissioner? Landis solved the problems with the acquittal of the Black Sox by acting as judge and jury. He took the law into his own hands, and distributed his version of justice in the most ancient of ways. Harold Seymour says that Landis "wielded not a sword of justice but an extra-legal scythe. He recognized no degrees of guilt but cut off from their livelihood seven ball players acquitted in a court of law and two others who were not even indicted." Landis was an "authoritarian personality not bothered by any hobgoblins or consistency."

Hugh Fullerton wrote, "I happen to know that Judge Landis has been keenly interested in the current stories of the World's Series. He has heard the entire story and was shocked and grieved."[99] This is well before he became commissioner. Fullerton felt that the gamblers would have told Landis in confidence all of the facts. The gamblers trusted Landis. If Landis would have heard testimony from the gamblers and especially Bill Burns, Landis would have had all of the facts months before the beginning of the 1920 season. Judge Kenesaw Mountain Landis is in the Baseball Hall of Fame, but Joseph Jefferson Jackson is not. Landis' reputation for integrity and wisdom has long since outrun his reputation for whimsicalness, cantankerousness, and extra-legality. He was "a federal judge with a reputation for willful independence equaled only by his flair for self promotion...a showboat judge."[100] I reiterate Bill Veeck, Jr.'s assertion that "…everybody did their best to cover up. *Everybody.* From the Commissioner (Ban Johnson) on down."[101] Harold Seymour contends that Landis did not save baseball. Attendance picked up sharply after World War I--before Landis entered the picture, and fans were captivated by Babe Ruth.[102] Is *the wrong man out*, and is *the wrong man in?*

CHAPTER 5

A Modern Day Trial of Shoeless Joe Jackson and Major League Baseball

This is a fictitious trial, and the questions and responses are derived from research of various sources. None of the responses, even those documented by footnotes unless quoted, are the words of the characters, living or deceased, portrayed in this trial. Those documented by footnotes can be researched in the given reference and page. The given testimony is, as much as possible, based on "facts" or the opinions of other authors as documented in footnotes and the bibliography.

Let me preface this trial by stating that I got my law degree from watching *Boston Legal*, so if you think this sounds a bit like Denny Crane and Alan Shore, you now know why. With all that said, let's have some fun and get this trial started.

Judge: The prosecutor will begin the opening arguments.

Prosecutor: Ladies and gentlemen of the jury, Major League baseball will show that Mr. Joseph Jefferson Jackson, also known as "Shoeless" Joe Jackson, was banned for life from Major League baseball with just cause. Mr. Jackson accepted $5,000 during or after the 1919 World Series for his willingness to partake in throwing the World Series to the Cincinnati Red Legs. He also signed a confession and waived immunity from prosecution for his part in the "fixing" of the 1919 World Series. Judge Kenesaw Mountain Landis had no other choice than to ban "Shoeless" Joe from baseball for all time, and the ensuing commissioners of baseball had to uphold that decision. Judge Landis had a duty and mandate to restore the good name of baseball, and he started by banning those involved in the "Big Fix" from baseball for life. Were it not for the actions of Judge Landis, baseball may not have survived as a great American institution, the great American game and pasttime.

Defense: The prosecutor paints a rosy picture of Judge Landis and the great American institution of baseball, but he has forgotten to mention the thorns on the rose, namely, the magnates of baseball, the Baseball Hall of Fame, and Judge Landis himself. Yes, "Shoeless" Joe admits receiving $5,000 dollars during or after the 1919 World Series, but the receipt of that money is an issue of debate. Furthermore, Mr. Jackson's confession was obtained through shady dealings of Mr. Comiskey and Mr. Austrian, Mr. Comiskey's attorney, "lost" conveniently, and then "found" conveniently. Also, Mr. Jackson swore under oath to the Grand Jury that he played to the best of his ability in the 1919 World Series, a fact I will prove. Finally, I will attempt to show that there are certain members of the Hall of Fame that should be removed.

Judge: Mr. Prosecutor call your first witness.

Prosecutor: I call Judge Kenesaw Mountain Landis to the stand.

Judge Landis is sworn in and states his name for the record.

Prosecutor: Judge Landis, were you the commissioner of Major League Baseball at the time the 1919 World Series was played?

Landis: No. I was not appointed Commissioner of Major League Baseball until early 1921.

Prosecutor: Who appointed you?

Landis: The owners of the Major League teams at the time.

Prosecutor: What was your occupation before assuming the job as Commissioner?

Landis: I was a federal judge.

Prosecutor: Do you know why you were chosen to be the Commissioner of baseball?

Landis: I am not entirely sure, but I assume it was because of my record as a federal judge.

Prosecutor: Were you given any guidelines, instructions, or directions by those who appointed you?

Landis: I was told to "clean up" baseball.

Prosecutor: What did they mean by "clean up" baseball?

Landis: The 1919 World Series scandal broke open in August 1920, gamblers were infesting baseball, and the owners feared that baseball would lose its appeal to the American public. The magnates of baseball gave me unconditional power and control to remove the gamblers and crooked ball players and restore the good name of Baseball.

Prosecutor: So, on August 4, 1921, you banned eight White Sox players and Fred McMullin from baseball for life. Why did you deem that a necessary action especially after the eight White Sox players were exonerated?

Landis: "Regardless of the verdict of juries, no player that throws a ball game, no player that entertains proposal of promises to throw a game, no player that sits in conference with a bunch of crooked players and gamblers where the ways and means to throwing games are discussed, and does not promptly tell his club about it, will ever play professional baseball."

Prosecutor: What proof did you have that the nine players "threw a ball game, entertained proposal of promises to throw a game, sat in conference with a bunch of crooked players and gamblers where the ways and means to throwing games are discussed, and did not promptly tell his club about it"?

Landis: There were signed confessions to the Grand Jury by three of the players--Misters Cicotte, Williams, and Jackson, and testimony of the other five Chicago White Sox involvement or admission of guilt by some.

Prosecutor: No further questions, Your Honor.

Judge: Your witness, Defense.

Defense: Judge Landis, you stated that you were a federal judge. Are you proud of your record when you sat on the bench?

Landis: Of course.

Defense: Weren't a number of your verdicts overturned by a higher court?

Landis: A few, I guess.

Defense: Didn't you endear yourself to baseball when you let an antitrust suit against Major League Baseball by the Federal League continue until the Federal League went bankrupt?

Landis: The Federal League went bankrupt, but I don't know that that was my fault.

Defense: What is your stand on antitrust?

Landis: I am a firm believer in breaking trusts.

Defense: But you delayed long enough for the Federal League's anti-trust suit against Major League Baseball to wither on the vine until the Federal League was bankrupt and unable to sustain anymore legal fees. Being vehement about dissolving trusts, do you think that, if you would have acted sooner, you could have ruled on the Federal League's anti-trust suit.

Landis: I had to allow all motions and evidence to be entered in order to make a fair decision.

Defense: You are one hell of a trust buster, Judge Landis. Let's discuss Joseph Jefferson Jackson whom you seemed to judge without considering all of the evidence, contrary to your dealing with the Federal League.

Prosecutor: Objection.

Judge: Sustained.

Defense: Judge Landis, do you have any evidence that Mr. Jackson threw any ball games?

Landis: Well, no.

Defense: In fact, Mr. Jackson testified under oath that he played to the best of his ability, did he not?

Landis: Yes.

Defense: Is there any evidence that Mr. Jackson entertained "proposal of promises to throw a game"?

Landis: No.

Defense: Is there any evidence that Mr. Jackson sat "in conference with a bunch of crooked players and gamblers where the ways and means to throwing games are discussed"?

Landis: No.

Defense: As a matter of fact, there is no evidence ever showing that Mr. Jackson was in on any discussions with crooked players and gamblers to throw ball games? There is no proof that Mr. Jackson was ever in a room with the characters when they plotted to throw the World Series?

Landis: I don't know.

Defense: Is there any evidence that Mr. Jackson did "not promptly tell his club about it"?

Landis: No.

Defense: As a matter of fact, there is a great deal of evidence to suggest that Mr. Jackson tried to tell Mr. Comiskey and Mr. Austrian, but he was dismissed?

Landis: I don't know.

Defense: There is a great deal of evidence that suggests that Mr. Jackson tried to give $5,000 to Mr. Comiskey, but he was dismissed by Mr. Grabiner, Mr. Comiskey's secretary.

Landis: I don't know.

Defense: Judge Landis, is our system of justice based on "innocent until proven guilty?"

Landis: Yes.

Defense: So, in Mr. Jackson's case, it was guilty although proven innocent.

Prosecutor: Objection.

Judge: Sustained.

Defense: Judge Landis, you liked being Commissioner without restraint. You could be judge and jury.

Prosecutor: Objection.

Judge: Sustained.

Defense: You became aware of Misters Ty Cobb and Tris Speaker allegedly throwing games between the Detroit Tigers and the Cleveland Indians in 1919. Mr. Risberg, one of the ring leaders in the 1919 "Fix" paid them $1,100 to throw some games. It was proven that the Tigers got the money. What did you do about that?

Landis: "It was an act of impropriety, reprehensible and censurable, but not an act of criminality."

Defense: You called it a gift and not a bribe, correct?

Landis: I decided that it was a gift.

Defense: A gift given after the Tigers had already lost? Why would anyone give a gift to the Tigers for something that had already happened unless it was to pay off a bribe?

Landis: I don't know.

Defense: You used the White Sox to prove your discretionary power and to solidify your position as Commissioner even though you violated the foundation of our legal system: "innocent until proven guilty."

Prosecutor: Objection.

Judge: Sustained.

Defense: You ruined Mr. Jackson's career for your own personal gain.

Prosecutor: Objection.

Judge: Sustained.

Defense: Judge Landis, did you ban Ray Fisher from baseball for refusing to take a pay cut of $1,000 and requesting a release from the

Cincinnati Reds to accept a position as the football coach and freshman baseball coach at the University of Michigan?

Landis: Yes.

Defense: That was another of your decisions that was overturned, wasn't it?

Landis: I suppose.

Defense: By Commissioner of Baseball Bowie Kuhn?

Landis: Yes.

Defense: But Mr. Kuhn wasn't very consistent either, was he? He suspended Denny McLain for three months and put him on probation for alleged bookmaking, correct?

Landis: Yes, but the alleged bookmaking was never proven.

Defense: You enjoyed being judge and jury, didn't you?

Prosecutor: Objection.

Judge: Over ruled.

Landis: No. I dealt with each situation as I best saw fit.

Defense: Are you aware that in 1993 San Francisco's Court of Historical Review ruled that Joseph Jefferson Jackson should be reinstated by Major League Baseball?

Landis: Yes.

Defense: Another decision overturned.

Landis: That is a non-binding, legal decision.

Defense: Nonetheless, a court of review disagrees with another of your decisions. Judge Landis, you would like to take credit for baseball making a comeback after the 1919 scandal wouldn't you?

Landis: Some.

Defense: But the truth of the matter is that baseball was making a comeback because the war was over, the ball was livelier, and America was infatuated by George Herman "Babe" Ruth during the 1920 season?

Landis: Well, that surely had something to do with it, I suppose.

Defense: You were inducted into the Baseball Hall of Fame, weren't you?

Landis: Yes.

Defense: Unbelievable! Violating the fundamental precept of our system of justice to ruin the careers of proven innocent men for your own advancement. No further questions.

Prosecutor: Objection.

Judge: Sustained.

Judge: Mr. Prosecutor, please call your next witness.

Prosecutor: The prosecution calls Mr. Charles Comiskey.

Mr. Comiskey is sworn in and states his name for the record.

Prosecutor: Mr. Comiskey, in 1919 what was your occupation?

Comiskey: I was the owner of the Chicago White Sox of the American Baseball League.

Prosecutor: Did Mr. Joseph Jackson ever try to give you $5,000 that he received during or after the 1919 World Series?

Comiskey: No.

Prosecutor: Did you have any knowledge of a conspiracy by your ballplayers to throw the 1919 World Series?

Comiskey: I heard rumors. There were a lot of rumors flying around about a fix. Heck, there were rumors about a fix of the 1918 World Series.

Prosecutor: What did you do about the rumors?

Comiskey: I hired detectives and offered a reward of $10,000 for information proving that my players were in on a fix.

Prosecutor: And what was the result of that investigation?

Comiskey: "There is always some scandal of some kind following a big sporting event like the World Series. These yarns are manufactured out of whole cloth and grow out of bitterness due to losing wagers."

Prosecutor: Did you ever confront Mr. Byron Bancroft "Ban" Johnson, the American League president at the time, that there was a rumor of a "fix"?

Comiskey: Yes, John Hydler, the National League president, and I went to Ban and told him that my manager, Kid Gleason, had received some telegrams after the first game of the 1919 World Series stating that there were rumors of a fix.

Prosecutor: And what did Mr. Johnson do?

Comiskey: Nothing. He accused me of crying like a "whipped cur."

Prosecutor: When did you find out for certain that your players were in on the "Big Fix"?

Comiskey: When Cicotte confessed.

Prosecutor: To you?

Comiskey: To me and to Mr. Austrian.

Prosecutor: And what did you do?

Comiskey: When Misters Williams and Jackson were implicated by Mr. Cicotte, I called Williams and Jackson and had them sign confessions like Mr. Cicotte did.

Prosecutor: What did you do with the confessions?

Comiskey: I gave them to the Mr. Replogle, the prosecutor for Cook County Grand Jury.

Prosecutor: No further questions.

Defense: Mr. Comiskey, you stated that you learned of the "fix" after game one of the 1919 World Series. Are you certain that you did not know about it before then?

Comiskey: I am pretty certain.

Defense: Did you or didn't you?

Comiskey: I don't think that I did.

Defense: Mr. Comiskey, I will later call a witness that will testify that you "had an inkling of what was going on from the very first game of the 1919 World Series."

Comiskey: Well I might have, but there were only rumors.

Defense: You stated the Mr. Jackson never tried to give you $5,000. Did he try to give anyone on your staff the $5,000?

Comiskey: I believe that he tried to give it to Mr. Grabiner.

Defense: Do you know what Mr. Grabiner did?

Comiskey: I don't think he did anything.

Defense: You testified that you hired investigators and offered a reward for information proving that some of your players were throwing the 1919 World Series. When did you hire the investigators?

Comiskey: I believe it was after the Series was over.

Defense: And you testified that you never had any proof of a "fix"?

Comiskey: Correct.

Defense: Did you learn the names of the St. Louis gamblers that were in on the "fix"?

Comiskey: Yes.

Defense: What did you do with that information?

Comiskey: Nothing.

Defense: Why not?

Comiskey: I didn't think that small time gamblers could fix a World Series.

Defense: It looks like maybe they did. Let's talk about Mr. Ban Johnson. Were you two friends?

Comiskey: We were initially, but later we had our differences.

Defense: At the time of the 1919 World Series were you two friends?

Comiskey: No.

Defense: Were you and Judge Landis friends?

Comiskey: Yes.

Defense: As a matter of fact, you were instrumental in getting Judge Landis appointed Commissioner of Major League Baseball which left Mr. Johnson without a job?

Comiskey: I helped get Judge Landis appointed, yes.

Defense: Let's focus on the confessions of Misters Cicotte, Williams, and Jackson. Who was in the room when the confessions were signed?

Comiskey: The player, me, and Mr. Austrian.

Defense: And please tell us who Mr. Austrian is.

Comiskey: He is my attorney--for me and the White Sox.

Defense: Did the players sign any other documents?

Comiskey: Yes. They signed waivers of immunity.

Defense: Waivers of immunity from prosecution for their testimony?

Comiskey: Yes.

Defense: So the players signed confessions for the Grand Jury and then waived their rights to immunity from prosecution for their testimony?

Comiskey: Yes.

Defense: And there was no one else in the room?

Comiskey: No.

Defense: The players were not represented by counsel?

Comiskey: No, they were not.

Defense: Do you know if Mr. Jackson was able to read either of the documents?

Comiskey: No, Mr. Jackson could not read.

Defense: So, none of the ballplayers had legal representation, they signed documents prepared by you and your attorney, and Mr. Jackson signed a document that he couldn't read. Who read the document to Mr. Jackson?

Comiskey: Mr. Austrian explained it to Mr. Jackson.

Defense: He explained to Mr. Jackson that he could go to jail because of his testimony, and Mr. Jackson said, "No problem. I'll indict myself and let you use my words against me to put me in jail?"

Prosecutor: Objection.

Judge: Sustained.

Defense: And what happened to those sworn confessions after the Grand Jury indicted the ballplayers and before the trial?

Comiskey: I don't know.

Defense: Were they used in the ballplayers' trial?

Comiskey: No.

Defense: Why not?

Comiskey: They were lost.

Defense: Lost? Were they ever found?

Comiskey: Yes.

Defense: When?

Comiskey: In 1924 at a civil trial brought by Mr. Jackson.

Defense: What was Mr. Jackson's complaint, and who was it against?

Comiskey: It was against me for back wages on his contract from 1920.

Defense: Who produced Mr. Jackson's confession?

Comiskey: Mr. Austrian.

Defense: Your attorney, Mr. Austrian? How did he get them?

Comiskey: I don't know.

Defense: The lost confessions were not available for the ballplayers' trial, but all of sudden your attorney just happens to locate them to defend you in a civil trial. I smell something rotten, but that's a familiar smell around baseball in 1919, especially the magnates of baseball.

Prosecutor: Objection.

Judge: Sustained.

Defense: I have no more questions at this time, but I would like to call this witness after the prosecution rests.

Judge: You may step down. Prosecution, call your next witness.

Prosecutor: I could parade all of the baseball commissioners from Judge Landis to Mr. Selig to testify why they upheld Judge Landis' decision, but I believe that would be a waste of the court's time, and, if Defense has no objection to allowing the fact that they agreed with Judge Landis, I will rest.

Judge: Defense, any objection?

Defense: None except for noting that Mr. Selig has stated that he would look into Mr. Jackson's case and that Commissioner Chandler, after he left office, stated that Mr. Jackson should be reinstated into Major League Baseball.

Judge: Prosecution, any objection?

Prosecutor: No, your Honor.

Judge: Defense, you may call your first witness.

Defense: I would like to recall Mr. Comiskey.

Judge: Mr. Comiskey, you are still under oath.

Defense: Mr. Comiskey, what was your relationship like with your players?

Comiskey: Boss-laborer.

Defense: Were you a benevolent boss or more of a dictator?

Comiskey: I was the owner, the boss.

Defense: And that 1919 White Sox team was considered the best in Major League Baseball wasn't it?

Comiskey: Yes.

Defense: How did the pay of your players compare with the league?

Comiskey: I don't know.

Defense: Let me show you some figures. In 1919, you paid Mr. Jackson $6,000 and Ty Cobb was making $20,000. And "Shoeless" Joe was in a continuous battle with Mr. Cobb for the batting title each year. Will you agree with that?

Comiskey: Yes.

Defense: Your manager, Mr. Gleason, came to you during the 1919 season on behalf of the team asking for a pay increase, did he not?

Comiskey: Yes.

Defense: And what did you do?

Comiskey: I did nothing.

Defense: And Mr. Cicotte had an incentive clause in his contract giving him a bonus if he won 30 games, but you told Mr. Gleason to hold him out at the end of the season to keep him from getting the bonus, didn't you?

Comiskey: I held him out because the staff was tired, and we needed our pitchers rested for the Series.

Defense: What did you pay your players for meals per day?

Comiskey: Three dollars.

Defense: And what was the going rate for most Major League players?

Comiskey: I'm not sure.

Defense: It was four dollars. Did you charge your players fifty cents to clean their uniforms?

Comiskey: Yes.

Defense: Was that customary?

Comiskey: I don't know.

Defense: It wasn't. Did you promise your players a bonus for winning the 1917 pennant?

Comiskey: Yes.

Defense: And how much was that bonus?

Comiskey: Champagne.

Defense: Stale champagne that was left over from the party for the press. To quote Mr. Ring Lardner, "It tasted like stale piss." You're a real cheap skate, aren't you, Mr. Comiskey?

Prosecutor: Objection.

Judge: Sustained. Sir, be very careful with your theatrics.

Defense: Mr. Comiskey, would you consider yourself a cheap skate?

Comiskey: No. I paid the players what they agreed to in their contracts.

Defense: Except for Mr. Jackson who had to take you to court for his pay. What was the outcome of that trial?

Comiskey: The jury found in favor of Mr. Jackson, but the judge ruled that I would not have to pay Mr. Jackson because he perjured himself in his trial.

Defense: Perjured himself because the "lost" confessions somehow appeared in your attorney's briefcase during the trial. That was convenient wasn't it? Did you withhold the loser's share of the 1919 World Series from some of your players, namely, the ones that were implicated in throwing the World Series?

Comiskey: Yes.

Defense: Did you say that you would suspend any player that tried to throw the World Series?

Comiskey: Yes.

Defense: But, in fact, you gave Cicotte a $5,000 raise and Williams and Felsch $3,000 raises for the 1920 season?

Comiskey: Yes.

Defense: And when Mr. Jackson refused to play for $6,000 in 1920, you sent Mr. Grabiner to Savannah to offer Mr. Jackson a $2,000 raise, true?

Comiskey: Yes.

Defense: And when Mr. Jackson would not sign the contract until his wife read it to him, Mr. Grabiner pressured Mr. Jackson into signing the contract, right?

Comiskey: All I know is that Mr. Grabiner returned to Chicago with a signed contract for $8,000 a year.

Defense: The same contract that you welched on and Mr. Jackson had to take you to court to collect. We'll see what Mr. Grabiner has to say when we put him on the stand. Just before the 1920 season ended, you suspended the eight ballplayers that were allegedly in on the "fix" when the lid began to blow and gamblers were ready to talk, correct?

Comiskey: Yes.

Defense: But, before that, you had no real proof that there were some players who threw the Series, right? And I remind you that you are under oath.

Comiskey: I had no real proof.

Defense: Did Mr. Jackson come to you before game one of the Series and try to tell you that a "fix" was on?

Comiskey: I don't think so. Maybe he did. I can't remember.

Defense: Wasn't Mr. Hugh Fullerton in your office when Mr. Jackson told you?

Comiskey: I don't remember.

Defense: I guess we'll see what Mr. Fullerton has to say when I put him on the stand. Maybe that will jog your memory. Is it true that you ignored the rumors and facts because you had a great team, and you thought that they could win a lot of pennants and World Series if the rumors and facts just went away?

Comiskey: No.

Defense: And when the lid blew, you decided to save face and help Landis clean up baseball?

Comiskey: That's not true.

Defense: Poor Mr. Comiskey, the whipped cur, betrayed by his beloved ballplayers. Some people think that, if you treated your players fairly, the "Big Fix" would never have happened. I suppose you disagree.

Comiskey: I certainly do.

Defense: And you, too, are in the Hall of Fame. Maybe it should be renamed the Hall of Shame.

Defense: Do you think that Mr. Jackson played to the best of his ability in the 1919 World Series.

Comiskey: Yes.

Defense: No further questions.

Judge: Your witness Mr. Prosecutor.

Prosecutor: No questions, your Honor.

Defense: I would now like to call Mr. Harry Grabiner to the stand.

Mr. Grabiner is sworn in and states his name for the record.

Defense: Mr. Grabiner, I am going to show you exhibit 1, your diary. Please read the first excerpt that I have noted.

Grabiner: "…beyond any doubt, the White Sox front office had more than some inkling of what was going on from the very first game of the 1919 World Series."

Defense: Does that include Mr. Comiskey?

Grabiner: Yes.

Defense: Did Mr. Jackson come to your office after the 1919 World Series?

Grabiner: Yes.

Defense: Why did he come to your office?

Grabiner: He had $5,000 that he said he got from Lefty Williams.

Defense: What happened to the money?

Grabiner: I don't know.

Defense: Did you advise Mr. Jackson on what to do with the money?

Grabiner: Yes. I told him to go to Savannah and keep it because "Cicotte, Williams, and the others wrongfully used his name."[103]

Defense: Did Mr. Comiskey send you to Savannah to get Mr. Jackson to sign his 1920 contract?

Grabiner: Yes.

Defense: Did he sign willingly?

Grabiner: After we spoke a while he did.

Defense: Spoke, or did you lay it on the line that he better sign?

Grabiner: We had discussions.

Defense: Did Mrs. Jackson have an opportunity to read the contract for Joe?

Grabiner: No. I was in a hurry to get back to Chicago.

Defense: Would you be surprised if Mr. Jackson has a different take on what happened that day?

Grabiner: He will probably see it from his perspective.

Defense: I'll bet he will. No further questions.

Judge: Your witness Mr. Prosecutor.

Prosecutor: No questions, your Honor.

Judge: Defense, call your next witness.

Defense: The defense calls Mr. Hugh Fullerton.

Mr. Fullerton is sworn in and states his name for the record.

Defense: Mr. Fullerton, what is your occupation?

Fullerton: I am a sports writer.

Defense: Did you cover the 1919 World Series?

Fullerton: Yes.

Defense: Did you hear of any rumors that the World Series was going to be thrown by the White Sox?

Fullerton: Yes, they were everywhere.

Defense: Did you tell anyone about the alleged "Fix".

Fullerton: Yes. I told Christy Mathewson and Charles Comiskey.

Defense: When did you tell Mr. Comiskey?

Fullerton: Before game one of the 1919 World Series.[104]

Defense: What did Mr. Comiskey do?

Fullerton: He got angry and told me that he had already heard about it.

Defense: Then what did you do?

Fullerton: I told Mr. Ban Johnson.

Defense: What did Mr. Johnson do?

Fullerton: He scoffed and said it was just Commy squealing.[105]

Defense: Did you observe the play of the World Series by the Chicago White Sox?

Fullerton: Yes, me and Christy Mathewson.

Defense: And what did you and Mr. Mathewson ascertain.

Fullerton: We noted seven questionable plays by the White Sox.

Defense: After the Series, what did you conclude?

Fullerton: "…an evil minded person might believe the stories that have been circulated during the series. The fact is that this series was lost in the first game, and lost through overconfidence."

Defense: But later you persisted in claiming that there was a "fix"?

Fullerton: Yes, and I was pretty much black balled by the press, but more stories started to surface from gamblers and players. Ray Schalk made some strong statements right after the Series and said that seven of the White Sox would not return.

Defense: Was Mr. Jackson one of the seven?

Fullerton: I don't think so.

Defense: Were you in Mr. Comiskey's office when Mr. Jackson came to him with the suspicion of a fix?

Fullerton: Yes.

Defense: Mr. Comiskey was your friend, wasn't he?

Fullerton: Yes. He was instrumental in my getting into sports writing.

Defense: And you certainly owe him a debt for that, don't you?

Fullerton: Yes.

Defense: And you wouldn't say anything or make up any story to hurt Mr. Comiskey, would you?

Fullerton: No.

Defense: No further questions.

Judge: Your witness Mr. Prosecutor.

Prosecutor: Mr. Fullerton, are you and Mr. Comiskey friends now?

Fullerton: Not really.

Prosecutor: What happened?

Fullerton: When I began to pursue the "Big Fix", Mr. Comiskey seemed to separate himself from me. He broke off contact.

Prosecutor: You're pretty proud to be the one history said broke open the scandal of the 1919 World Series, aren't you?

Fullerton: That's nothing to be proud of. It was a terrible time in American history and for baseball. I only reported.

Prosecutor: But you sure became famous, didn't you?

Fullerton: I guess so, but I was also vindicated.

Prosecutor: And you got back at Mr. Comiskey, too. Sweet deal.

Fullerton: I owe Mr. Comiskey a great deal, and I would never do anything intentionally to hurt Mr. Comiskey, but someone needed to look at baseball and gambling and separate the two, and, if exposing the "Big Fix" did that, then I am proud of what I did.

Prosecutor: No further questions.

Judge: Defense, call your next witness.

Defense: I call Mr. Joseph Jefferson Jackson to the stand.

Mr. Jackson is sworn in and states his name for the record.

Defense: Mr. Jackson, Joe, "Shoeless" Joe, you have heard the testimony from Misters Comiskey and Grabiner and from Judge Landis. I am going to have you shed some light on some of the issues. First, and foremost, did you intentionally play below your ability at any time during the 1919 World Series?

Jackson: No, Sir. Never. I have said that time and again. Heck, I swore to it to the Grand Jury.

Defense: Did you inform Mr. Comiskey of the possibility of crooked ballplayers trying to throw the 1919 World Series to the Cincinnati Red Legs?

Jackson: Yes, Sir.

Defense: And what did Mr. Comiskey do?

Jackson: He sent me out of his office and did nothing.

Defense: What did you say to Mr. Comiskey?

Jackson: I went to Mr. Comiskey and begged him to take me out of the lineup…If there was something going on I knew the bench would be the safest place, but he wouldn't listen to me." Then, I tried to fake an illness to keep from playing in the first game of the Series, but Gleason, the manager, and Comiskey ordered me to play.

Defense: Did anyone ever threaten you if you said anything about the "fix"?

Jackson: Swede Risberg. He was big and mean.

Defense: Did you receive any money for the outcome of the 1919 World Series?

Jackson: Yes, Sir. I got $5,000.

Defense: How much were you promised?

Jackson: $20,000.

Defense: From whom?

Jackson: Chick Gandil.

Defense: And why did he promise you that money?

Jackson: Because he used my name to the gamblers, and he said that I might as well get something if they think that I am in with the guys planning to throw the Series.

Defense: Who actually gave you the $5,000?

Jackson: Lefty Williams.

Defense: What did Mr. Williams say?

Jackson: "One of these is for you, Joe. Some of the players sold the Series to a gambling clique. We told that clique that you would play crooked ball, too. There's $5,000 in the envelope. It's not all what we were promised, but it's better than getting nothing."

Defense: What did you say to Mr. Williams?

Jackson: I told Lefty that he "had a hell of a lot of nerve using my name in the affair."

Defense: Why did you keep the money?

Jackson: "I thought just this way, since that lousy so-called gambling outfit had used my name, I might as well have their money."[106]

Defense: "How did you know they used your name?"[107]

Jackson: "I had Williams' word on it."[108]

Defense: Did you know that you were a part of the "Fix"?

Jackson: No.

Defense: When did you learn that you were used to help set up the "Fix"?

Jackson: When Lefty handed me the money after the Series.[109]

Defense: What did you do with the $5,000?

Jackson: I tried to give it to Mr. Comiskey. I told Mr. Grabiner that I had the money and wanted to see Mr. Comiskey, but Mr. Grabiner said we know what you want. I showed him the money, and he told me to keep it and go home.

Defense: When was the next time that you saw Mr. Grabiner?

Jackson: When he came to Savannah to get me to sign my 1920 contract.

Defense: Why did he come to see you?

Jackson: Because I wasn't gonna play for $6,000. I wanted more money. Heck, Cobb, that S.O.B., was making $20,000, and I could hit as well as he could, and I sure was a better fielder.

Defense: What did Mr. Grabiner do?

Jackson: We went for a ride, and he finally said, "We've got the goods on Cicotte, Williams, and Gandil. We know who was guilty in throwing the Series. We know it all and how much each man got in being crooked. We know you discussed fixing the World Series with Gandil and that Williams gave you $5,000....Cicotte and Williams wrongfully used your name...You can take what I'm offering, or you can leave it. You well know that we can do anything we want with you, with any of you. You take it, or we kick you out of baseball."

Defense: So what did you do?

Jackson: I asked to have my wife read it to me before I signed it, but Mr. Grabiner said I sign it now because he was leaving for Chicago, and he didn't have the time for Mrs. Jackson to read it. So I signed it.

Defense: How did you sign it?

Jackson: I put my "X" on it.

Defense: Was there any other time that you signed papers for the White Sox without the benefit of Mrs. Jackson reading them to you.

Jackson: Yes, Sir. When Mr. Comiskey called me into his office with Mr. Austrian there. They said that they had the goods on us, and that I should sign a confession and some other paper. They told me to go ahead and sign the papers and that they would take care of me.

Defense: It sounds like they took care of you good. Did you have anyone, a lawyer, representing you?

Jackson: Mr. Austrian.

Defense: Mr. Austrian was representing you and Mr. Comiskey. Did they recommend that you get your own lawyer?

Jackson: No, Sir. They said that they would take care of me.

Defense: Did you ask for a lawyer?

Jackson: I didn't think that I needed another lawyer. I had Mr. Austrian.

Defense: Did you know what a waiver of immunity was?

Jackson: No, Sir. Mr. Austrian said to sign the papers, and he would take care of me.

Defense: You said you played to the best of your ability. Can you give some proof of that?

Jackson: I had the best batting average of anyone, made no errors, hit the only home run of the series, and threw out one player at the plate and may have throw out two more if Buck Weaver hadn't bobbled the ball and Cicotte deflected another.

Defense: Just to refresh your memory, you had a .375 batting average, the best of the Series; drove in 6 of the 17 White Sox runs, most on the White Sox and third behind Duncan and Roush of the Reds; had

12 hits, at the time a World Series record; and had a .563 slugging percentage. Does that sound about right?

Jackson: Yep.

Defense: You only hit .304 in the 1917 World Series that the White Sox won fair and square.

Jackson: Yes, Sir. At least there was no big hubbub about a fix. I wish I would have done better in that Series.

Defense: Joe, have you been inducted into any Hall of Fame?

Jackson: Yes, Sir. In 1951, I was inducted into the Cleveland Indians Baseball Hall of Fame.

Judge: Your witness, Mr. Prosecutor.

Prosecutor: Mr. Jackson, isn't it true that the home run you hit came when the last game of the series was out of reach?

Jackson: A game is never out of reach.

Prosecutor: Did you sign a confession to helping rig the 1919 World Series?

Jackson: Yes, Sir.

Prosecutor: Did you receive payment for helping rig the 1919 World Series?

Jackson: No, Sir. Lefty gave me $5,000 'cause they told the gamblers that I was in on it, because the gamblers said the "fix" would be off if I wasn't in on it.

Prosecutor: But you took $5,000?

Jackson: Yes, Sir. But like I said, I tried to give it to Mr. Comiskey.

Prosecutor: Just answer the question--did you take $5,000?

Jackson: Yes, Sir.

Prosecutor: And for some reason, you were promised $20,000?

Jackson: Yes, Sir.

Prosecutor: Did you tell Lefty Williams after the first day of the Series that it was a crooked deal all the way through, Gandil was not on the square with us?

Jackson: Yes, Sir.

Prosecutor: So you knew of the "Fix" at least after game 1?

Jackson: I guess so.

Prosecutor: No further questions.

Defense: But you knew that something wasn't right after game 1?

Jackson: Yes, Sir.

Defense: And you played to the best of your ability throughout the Series?

Jackson: I have always said that.

Defense: Joe, what did you do with the $5,000?

Jackson: Me and Katie, Mrs. Jackson, put it in the bank and left it there to draw interest.

Defense: Why did you do that?

Jackson: Because we didn't believe the money was ours.

Defense: What eventually happened to all of that money? It must have accrued a lot of interest in those many years.

Jackson: It was given to the American Heart Fund and the American Cancer Society.

Defense: No further questions.

Prosecutor: Mr. Jackson, your wife testified in the 1924 trial of Jackson vs. Comiskey that she used most of it to try to save your sister who was in the hospital. So what is the real story?

Jackson: We put it in the Chatham Bank in Savannah. A bank representative testified to that in that same trial.

Prosecutor: No further questions.

Defense: No further questions, Judge. The defense calls Mr. Eddie Collins.

Mr. Collins is sworn in and states his name for the record.

Defense: Mr. Collins, you were one of the quote "clean Sox" were you not?

Collins: Yes, Sir.

Defense: Were you ever associated with the Boston Red Sox?

Collins: Yes, I worked on the executive staff of the Boston Red Sox.

Defense: Did you have a conversation with Mr. Ted Williams about Joe Jackson and the alleged fixing of the 1919 World Series?

Collins: Yes, Sir, I did. I told him that Joe Jackson was not in on the "fix".

Defense: And what did Mr. Williams do after that?

Collins: He and Bob Feller and Hank Aaron started to solicit support to clear Joe's name and get him admitted into the Hall of Fame.

Defense: But that, like rumors of the "Big Fix" and steroids just fall on deaf ears, hoping it will just go away. Mr. Collins, when you were a baseball player, did you ever bet on a baseball game?

Collins: Yes, Sir, I did. I had Buck Weaver put $45 on a game for me.

Defense: Did you ever report that to anyone?

Collins: Yes, Sir, I did. I sent a letter to Judge Kenesaw Mountain Landis explaining it.

Defense: And what did Judge Landis do?

Collins: Nothing.

Defense: And are you in the Baseball Hall of Fame?

Collins: Yes, Sir, I am.

Defense: No further questions. Thank you, Mr. Collins.

Judge: Your witness Mr. Prosecutor.

Prosecutor: No questions, your Honor.

Judge: Defense, call your next witness.

Defense: I call Mr. J M Bennett.

Mr. Bennett is sworn in and states his name for the record.

Defense: Mr. Bennett, state your occupation.

Bennett: I am a mathematician.

Defense: In 1993, you published an article on Shoeless Joe Jackson. Could you please tell us about that.

Bennett: I used sabermetrics. In 1984 a colleague and I used statistics from two major league seasons to estimate the probability that the home team wins a game given the run differential (the home team runs minus visiting team runs), the half inning (top or bottom of the inning), the number of outs, and the on-base situation. Using these estimated probabilities, one can see how the probability of winning changes for each game event. One can measure a player's contribution to winning a game by summing the changes in win probabilities for each play in which the player has participated. This statistic, called the Player Game Percentage, was used by me to evaluate the batting performance of Joe Jackson who, as you know, was banished from baseball for allegedly throwing the 1919 World Series.

Defense: And what did you determine?

Bennett: A statistical analysis using the Player Game Percentage showed that Jackson played to his full potential during this series.

Defense: No further questions.

Judge: Your witness Mr. Prosecutor.

Prosecutor: As you stated, this analysis is a probability and not hard evidence.

Bennett: Yes, it's a probability matrix, but it does show that it is more probable that Mr. Jackson played to the best of his ability and not the contrary.

Prosecutor: No further questions.

Judge: Defense, call your next witness.

Defense: The defense calls the Curator of the Major League Baseball Hall of Fame.

The Curator is sworn in and states his name for the record.

Defense: Mr. Curator, please state your occupation.

Curator: I am the curator of the Baseball Hall of Fame.

Defense: Is anything related to "Shoeless" Joe Jackson in the Baseball Hall of Fame?

Curator: Yes, sir. There is a picture of him and his shoes.

Defense: Mr. Jackson's shoes are on display in the Baseball Hall of Fame?

Curator: Yes, Sir.

Defense: I guess that explains how he became known as "Shoeless" Joe. The Baseball Hall of Fame stole them. This is unbelievable. You have his shoes to make money on Mr. Jackson, but you will not let him into the Hall of Fame. Pretty typical of Major League Baseball. I have no more questions. The Defense rests.

Judge: Your witness Mr. Prosecutor.

Prosecutor: Mr. Curator, are you the one who decides who should be in the Hall of Fame?

Curator: No, Sir.

Prosecutor: Who does?

Curator: There is a committee comprised of the living members of the Hall of Fame and the Ford C. Frick and the J. G. Taylor Spink award winners. Nominees receiving 75 percent of the votes will be inducted into the Hall of Fame. This year, it took 62 votes to become an inductee.

Prosecutor: So, you have nothing to do with who is inducted into the Hall of Fame?

Curator: No, Sir.

Prosecutor: And, are you the one who chose to display Mr. Jackson's shoes.

Curator: No, Sir.

Prosecutor: And, to best of your knowledge, no one ripped them off of Mr. Jackson's feet or stole them from his locker?

Curator: No, Sir.

Prosecutor: No more questions.

Defense: Mr. Curator, to be on the ballot, a player must be in good standing with Major League Baseball, correct?

Curator: Yes, sir.

Defense: Therefore, Mr. Jackson cannot even be considered, correct?

Curator: Yes, sir.

Defense: No more questions. I call the Commissioner of Major League Baseball.

The Commissioner is sworn in and states his name for the record.

Defense: Mr. Commissioner, what is your current occupation?

Commissioner: I am the Commissioner of Major League Baseball.

Defense: Mr. Commissioner, who was the first Commissioner of Major League Baseball?

Commissioner: Judge Kenesaw Mountain Landis.

Defense: What is Judge Landis' connection to Mr. Joseph Jefferson Jackson?

Commissioner: Judge Kenesaw Mountain Landis banned Shoeless Joe Jackson from baseball because of Mr. Jackson's involvement in the throwing of the 1919 World Series.

Defense: Alleged throwing of the 1919 World Series. I believe that there is a lot of mixed evidence on that. How do you feel about that, and especially Mr. Jackson's involvement?

Commissioner: I believe that Mr. Jackson's involvement should be given a second look, but there is a lot of history and controversial evidence.

Defense: Did Commissioner Chandler, who followed Judge Landis as Commissioner of Baseball, have an opinion as to Mr. Jackson?

Commissioner: Yes. He felt that Mr. Jackson should be reinstated into Major League Baseball.

Defense: Why didn't Commissioner Chandler reinstate Mr. Jackson?

Commissioner: Because he made that statement after he had left office.

Defense: And when Mr. Vincent was Commissioner, what was his stand on Mr. Jackson?

Commissioner: He felt that we could not go back in time and play God with history.

Defense: But Mr. Vincent did play God. He erased the asterisk placed by Commissioner Ford Frick on Roger Maris' 61 home run season because it was in a season that had more games than the one in which Babe Ruth hit 60 home runs, correct?

Commissioner: Yes.

Defense: And Judge Landis certainly played God by banning the "Black Sox" who were found innocent in a court of law?

Prosecution: Objection.

Judge: Sustained.

Defense: Let me rephrase that. Did Judge Landis ban the ballplayers even though they were found innocent by a court of law?

Commissioner: Yes.

Defense: I would like to quote Judge Landis:

"Regardless of the verdict of juries, no player that throws a ball game, no player that entertains proposal of promises to throw a game, no player that sits in conference with a bunch of crooked players and gamblers where the ways and means to throwing games are discussed, and does not promptly tell his club about it, will ever play professional baseball."

Is there any evidence that Mr. Jackson "threw a ball game"?

Prosecution: Objection. Mr. Commissioner would not have all the legal evidence available.

Judge: Sustained.

Defense: Let me rephrase that. In your research, have you found any evidence that Mr. Jackson threw a ball game?

Commissioner: There is no hard evidence.

Defense: You have heard evidence and testimony here today. Did you see or hear any evidence that would lead you to believe that Mr. Jackson entertained proposals to throw or did throw any games.

Commissioner: Not that I heard, no.

Defense: I will assume that you have read the testimonies in the previous trials of Mr. Eddie Collins, Mr. Lefty Williams, and Mr. Abe Attel. They have testified, under oath, that Mr. Jackson had nothing to do with the throwing of the World Series, and, in fact, Mr. Williams has testified that Mr. Jackson's name was offered to the gamblers without Mr. Jackson's knowledge. Are you aware of that?

Commissioner: Yes.

Defense: Is there any evidence that Mr. Jackson sat in conference with a bunch of crooked players and gamblers where the ways and means to throwing games were discussed?

Commissioner: There is no hard evidence.

Defense: There is no evidence at all. Can you produce any?

Commissioner: No. But recent manuscripts from the 1919 and 1924 trials have surfaced and have not been reviewed by Major League Baseball.

Defense: And we have seen a lot of evidence pertaining to the 1919 and 1924 trials already. Is there any evidence that Mr. Jackson did not tell his club about the proposal of promises to throw a game, sitting in conference with a bunch of crooked players and gamblers where the ways and means to throwing games are discussed?

Commissioner: There is no hard evidence.

Defense: On the contrary, there is no hard evidence at all and a great deal of evidence showing that Mr. Jackson did report this to Mr. Comiskey. Isn't that true?

Commissioner: I would say so.

Defense: Would you like me to bring in a host of historical authors to testify that Mr. Comiskey did know about the "fix" as early as game two and from Mr. Jackson? Hell, Mr. Comiskey then reported it to Mr. Heydler.

Commissioner: No, that won't be necessary.

Defense: And you heard Mr. Comiskey testify that he, himself, thought that Mr. Jackson played to the best of his ability in the 1919 World Series, didn't you?

Commissioner: Yes.

Defense: And you heard Mr. Grabiner testify that he knew that Mr. Jackson reported that there was a "fix" after the first game, didn't you?

Commissioner: Yes.

Defense: Is Mr. Pete Rose banished from Baseball?

Commissioner: Yes.

Defense: Why?

Commissioner: Because he bet on baseball games.

Defense: Who did he bet on?

Commissioner: The Cincinnati Reds.

Defense: Wasn't that his team?

Commissioner: Yes.

Defense: Did Mr. Ty Cobb ever admit to betting on baseball?

Commissioner: I believe so.

Defense: Who did he bet on?

Commissioner: The Detroit Tigers, I think.

Defense: Wasn't that his team?

Commissioner: Yes.

Defense: Let me get this straight, Ty Cobb is in the Hall of Fame and in good standing with Baseball, but Pete Rose is out, but both bet on their own teams. Right?

Commissioner: Yes.

Defense: What's wrong with this picture? No further questions.

Judge: Prosecution?

Prosecution: No questions.

Judge: Closing arguments. Mr. Prosecutor.

Prosecutor: Major League Baseball is not on trial here. Joseph Jefferson Jackson is, and Mr. Jackson is guilty. He signed a confession to throwing the 1919 World Series which he later retracted, but he, nonetheless, confessed to helping throw the 1919 World Series. Judge Landis had no choice but to ban Mr. Jackson from baseball, and the ensuing Commissioners had no other choice than to uphold that decision. Mr. Jackson should not now or ever be reinstated by Major League Baseball. He was an unsavory part of the blackest day in the history of Major League Baseball, and he should bear the consequences of his actions.

Judge: Defense.

Defense: On the contrary, Major League Baseball *is* on trial here. The actions of cheap, stingy, conniving owners and god-playing commissioners have stripped Mr. Jackson of a right and honor which he truly deserves. Mr. Comiskey wrangled a confession out of "Shoeless" Joe who was not afforded the right to counsel of his choosing. Comiskey and his lawyer took advantage of Joe's illiteracy and got him to put his "X" on a document that he couldn't read. One that was "explained" to Joe by Comiskey's attorney. And Joe signed it because Misters Comiskey and Austrian said that they would "take care of" Joe. Mr. Comiskey used the same tactic to get Joe to sign his 1920 contract which Mr. Comiskey welched on. Mr. Comiskey didn't want Mrs. Jackson or an attorney for Mr. Jackson around to read the confession, waiver of immunity, or contract because Katie Jackson would never have allowed Joe to sign any of those documents. And Joe was not allowed his own counsel which Mr. Comiskey and Mr. Austrian knew were the legal and, should I say, honorable thing to do to protect Joe's rights, but they knew Joe trusted Mr. Comiskey and that Joe would believe them when they said that they would take care of him. They took care of him alright. They led him to slaughter. Joe trusted everybody, and that was his downfall.

And Comiskey and Austrian tried to cover it up. But when all hell broke loose, Mr. Comiskey chose to save his own neck at the expense of eight ballplayers and the Chicago White Sox. Comiskey may have coerced Joe to sign a confession because, if Joe were allowed to go free of guilt, his testimony would uncover Comiskey's cover up.

And Judge Landis, he was a real piece of work. A judge who carried out justice in the court and as commissioner of baseball as he saw fit…sometimes acting as judge and jury…like he did with Mr. Jackson. Two courts of law and a court of historical review have ruled in favor of Mr. Jackson, but Judge Landis and every commissioner since chose to ignore all of that. Why recognize the basis of our legal system, innocent until proven guilty? That just gets in the way of protecting Major League Baseball.

Did Judge Landis investigate the "Big Fix"? No, he just dealt out justice in the typical Landis way. The typical, inconsistent Landis way. A way that has been overturned by higher courts and fellow commissioners.

Mr. Jackson testified under oath and contends to this day that he played to the best of his ability. His statistics in the 1919 World Series underscore the fact that he played very well, better than anyone else on either team. The only pure statistic that he did not win was runs batted in, but he batted in a higher percentage of runs for his team than anyone else.

Then, there is the science of sabermetrics, a mathematical analysis of Mr. Jackson's play that shows that, in all probability, he played to the best of his ability. Now, we even have scientific proof that Mr. Jackson played to the best of his ability. What more does the Major League Baseball establishment want?

Major League Baseball *should* be on trial. Owners and commissioners sacrificed "Shoeless" Joe and others for their own personal gain. Landis secured his post as Commissioner of Baseball. He secured a place in history as the one who cleaned up Major League Baseball. And, yes, Mr. Comiskey lost one of the greatest teams in history, but he saved his own neck and his team, or what was left of it. He knew, or at least had a strong suspicion, that the 1919 Series was not on the up and up, but he chose to do nothing, unless you see the guise of an investigation as an attempt by Comiskey to get to the bottom of things and a reward which was never paid out in the face of testimony that some of the White Sox were on the take. Joe told him there was something going on. Comiskey's friend, Hugh Fullerton, told him there was something going on. His own manager told him there was something going on.

But he could have been banned from baseball by covering up the "Big Fix"…something he did try to do. But he is in the Hall of Fame.

And how contemptuous is Major League Baseball. They have the nerve to display "Shoeless" Joe Jackson's shoes in the Hall of Fame, but they won't reinstate him so that he could be reunited with his own footwear in the Hall of Fame where Joe truly belongs. They should send his shoes to the Cleveland Indians Hall of Fame where Joe Jackson has received his just reward…induction into that Hall of Fame. Maybe everyone would stop calling him "Shoeless" Joe.

We venerate Ty Cobb and Tris Speaker who may be way more guilty than Shoeless Joe Jackson. Judge Landis knew about Misters Cobb's and Speaker's betting on baseball games and did nothing. Judge Landis is in the Hall of Fame, and he is an honorable man. To quote Shakespeare, "So are they all, all honorable men."

In my opinion, the wrong man, Joseph Jefferson Jackson, and maybe a few others are out and the wrong men, Charles Albert Comiskey, Judge Kenesaw Mountain Landis, and probably a few others, are in.

Maybe Major League Baseball Commissioners should play "god" as they have in the past when it suited them and rectify these blatant mistakes. They probably won't be willing to remove anyone, but they sure should let Shoeless Joe Jackson join his shoes in the Baseball Hall of Fame.

BIBLIOGRAPHY

Asinof, Eliot, *Eight Men Out, The Black Sox and the 1919 World Series*, NY: Henry Holt and Company, Inc.: 1963.

Axelson, G.W., *"Commy" The Life Story of Charles A. Comiskey*, Jefferson (NC): McFarland and Company, Inc.: 2003.

Carney, Gene, *Burying the Black Sox, How Baseball's Cover-up of the 1919 World Series Fix Almost Succeeded*, Washington, D.C.: Potomac Books, Inc.: 2006.

Cook, William A., *The 1919 World Series, What Really Happened?*, Jefferson (NC): McFarland and Company, Inc.: 2001.

Dellinger, Susan, PhD, *Red Legs and Black Sox, Edd Roush and the Untold Story of the 1919 World Series*, Cincinnati: Emmis Books: 2006.

Frommer, Harvey, *Shoeless Joe and Ragtime Baseball*, Dallas: Taylor Publishing Company: 1992.

Gropman, Donald, *Say It Ain't So, Joe! The True Story of Shoeless Joe Jackson*, New York: Citadel Press: 1995.

Katcher, Leo, *The Big Bankroll, The Life and Times of Arnold RothStein*, New York: Da Capo Press: 1994.

Nathan, Daniel A., *Saying It's So, A Cultural History of the Black Sox Scandal*, Champaign (Il): The University of Illinois Press: 2003.

Pietrusza, David, *Judge and Jury, The Life and Times of Judge Kenesaw Mountain Landis*, South Bend, (In): Diamond Communications, Inc., 1998.

Footnotes

[1] *Saying It's So: A Cultural History of the Black Sox Scandal*, by Daniel A Nathan; pg115.

[2] *Saying It's So: a Cultural History of the Black Sox Scandal*, by Daniel A Nathan; pg5.

[3] *Saying It's So: A Cultural History of the Black Sox Scandal*, by Daniel A Nathan; pg108.

[4] *Burying the Black Sox*, by Gene Carney; pg 48.

[5] *Burying the Black Sox*, by Gene Carney; pg 58.

[6] *Burying the Black Sox*, by Gene Carney; pg 44.

[7] *Red Sox and Black Legs*, Susan Dellinger; pg. 188.

[8] *Burying the Black Sox*, by Gene Carney; pg 44.

[9] *Burying the Black Sox*, by Gene Carney; pg 241.

[10] *Red Sox and Black Legs*, Susan Dellinger; pg. 309.

[11] *Red Sox and Black Legs*, Susan Dellinger; pg. 309.

[12] *Red Sox and Black Legs*, Susan Dellinger; pg. 321.

[13] *Red Sox and Black Legs*, Susan Dellinger; pg. 335.

[14] *The 1919 World Series, What Really Happened,* by William A. Cook; pg107.

[15] *Saying It's So: A Cultural History of the Black Sox Scandal,* by Daniel A Nathan; pg30.

[16] *Saying It's So: A Cultural History of the Black Sox Scandal,* by Daniel A Nathan; pg11.

[17] *Saying It's So: A Cultural History of the Black Sox Scandal,* by Daniel A Nathan; pg111.

[18] *Saying It's So: A Cultural History of the Black Sox Scandal,* by Daniel A Nathan; pg130.

[19] *Saying It's So: A Cultural History of the Black Sox Scandal,* by Daniel A Nathan; pg114.

[20] *Burying the Black Sox,* by Gene Carney; pg 124.

[21] *Saying It's So: A Cultural History of the Black Sox Scandal,* by Daniel A Nathan; pg108.

[22] *Saying It's So: A Cultural History of the Black Sox Scandal,* by Daniel A Nathan; pg18.

[23] *Burying the Black Sox,* by Gene Carney; pg 101.

[24] *Saying It's So: A Cultural History of the Black Sox Scandal,* by Daniel A Nathan; pg17.

[25] *Red Sox and Black Legs,* Susan Dellinger; pg. 155.

[26] *The 1919 World Series, What Really Happened,* by William A. Cook; pg7.

[27] *Burying the Black Sox*, by Gene Carney; pg. 98.

[28] *Burying the Black Sox*, by Gene Carney; pg 100.

[29] *Saying It's So: A Cultural History of the Black Sox Scandal*, by Daniel A Nathan; pg17.

[30] *Burying the Black Sox*, by Gene Carney; pg 188.

[31] *Burying the Black Sox*, by Gene Carney; pg 188.

[32] *Saying It's So: A Cultural History of the Black Sox Scandal*, by Daniel A Nathan; pg107.

[33] *Saying It's So: A Cultural History of the Black Sox Scandal*, by Daniel A Nathan; pg112.

[34] *Saying It's So: A Cultural History of the Black Sox Scandal*, by Daniel A Nathan; pg111 and 112.

[35] *Burying the Black Sox*, by Gene Carney; pgxiii.

[36] *Red Legs and Black Sox*, by Susan Dellinger; pg 132 & 133.

[37] *Saying It's So: A Cultural History of the Black Sox Scandal*, by Daniel A Nathan; pg137-138.

[38] *Saying It's So: A Cultural History of the Black Sox Scandal*, by Daniel A Nathan; pg189.

[39] *Burying the Black Sox*, by Gene Carney; pg 65.

[40] *Burying the Black Sox*, by Gene Carney; pg 181.

[41] *Burying the Black Sox*, by Gene Carney; pg 287.

[42] *Saying It's So: A Cultural History of the Black Sox Scandal*, by Daniel A Nathan; pg203.

[43] *Burying the Black Sox*, by Gene Carney; pg 64.

[44] *Burying the Black Sox*, by Gene Carney; pg 69.

[45] *Burying the Black Sox*, by Gene Carney; pg 122.

[46] *Burying the Black Sox*, by Gene Carney; pg 71.

[47] *Burying the Black Sox*, by Gene Carney; pg 71.

[48] *Burying the Black Sox*, by Gene Carney; pg 71.

[49] *The 1919 World Series, What Really Happened,* by William A. Cook; pg15.

[50] *Shoeless Joe Jackson and Ragtime Baseball*, by Harvey Frommer; pg 96.

[51] *Burying the Black Sox*, by Gene Carney; pg 62.

[52] *The 1919 World Series, What Really Happened,* by William A. Cook; pg132.

[53] *Burying the Black Sox*, by Gene Carney; pg 178.

[54] The American Statistician, Nov 1993, Vol 47, #4 J M Bennett, *Did Shoeless Joe Jackson Throw the 1919 World Series?"* pg 241-250.

[55] *Red Sox and Black Legs*, Susan Dellinger; pg. 293.

[56] *Burying the Black Sox*, by Gene Carney; pg 202.

[57] *Burying the Black Sox*, by Gene Carney; pg 71.

[58] *The 1919 World Series, What Really Happened*, by William A. Cook; pg107.

[59] *Saying It's So: A Cultural History of the Black Sox Scandal*, by Daniel A Nathan; pg4.

[60] *Burying the Black Sox*, by Gene Carney; pg 5.

[61] *Burying the Black Sox*, by Gene Carney; pg 203.

[62] *Saying It's So: A Cultural History of the Black Sox Scandal*, by Daniel A Nathan; pg190.

[63] *Burying the Black Sox*, by Gene Carney; pg 67.

[64] *Burying the Black Sox*, by Gene Carney; pg 10.

[65] *Burying the Black Sox*, by Gene Carney; pg 64.

[66] *Burying the Black Sox*, by Gene Carney; pg 198.

[67] *Saying It's So: A Cultural History of the Black Sox Scandal*, by Daniel A Nathan; pg3.

[68] *Saying It's So: A Cultural History of the Black Sox Scandal*, by Daniel A Nathan; pg3.

[69] *Saying It's So: A Cultural History of the Black Sox Scandal*, by Daniel A Nathan; pg119.

[70] *Burying the Black Sox*, by Gene Carney; pg 43.

[71] *Burying the Black Sox*, by Gene Carney; pg 101-2.

[72] *Red Sox and Black Legs*, Susan Dellinger; pg. 302.

[73] *Red Sox and Black Legs*, Susan Dellinger; pg. 335.

[74] *Red Sox and Black Legs*, Susan Dellinger; pg. 319.

[75] *Burying the Black Sox*, by Gene Carney; pg 43.

[76] *Burying the Black Sox*, by Gene Carney; pg 8.

[77] *Burying the Black Sox*, by Gene Carney; pg 9.

[78] *Burying the Black Sox*, by Gene Carney; pg 11.

[79] *Burying the Black Sox*, by Gene Carney; pg 105.

[80] *Burying the Black Sox*, by Gene Carney; pg 8.

[81] *Saying It's So: A Cultural History of the Black Sox Scandal*, by Daniel A Nathan; pg119.

[82] *Burying the Black Sox*, by Gene Carney; pg 38.

[83] *Burying the Black Sox*, by Gene Carney; pg 38.

[84] *Burying the Black Sox*, by Gene Carney; pg 2.

[85] *Burying the Black Sox*, by Gene Carney; pg 242.

[86] *Saying It's So: A Cultural History of the Black Sox Scandal*, by Daniel A Nathan; pg107.

[87] *Saying It's So: A Cultural History of the Black Sox Scandal*, by Daniel A Nathan; pg116.

[88] *Saying It's So: A Cultural History of the Black Sox Scandal*, by Daniel A Nathan; pg126.

[89] *Saying It's So: A Cultural History of the Black Sox Scandal*, by Daniel A Nathan; pg126.

[90] *Saying It's So: A Cultural History of the Black Sox Scandal*, by Daniel A Nathan; pg136.

[91] *Red Sox and Black Legs*, Susan Dellinger; pg. 300.

[92] *Burying the Black Sox*, by Gene Carney; pg 61.

[93] *Burying the Black Sox*, by Gene Carney; pg 211.

[94] *Saying It's So: A Cultural History of the Black Sox Scandal*, by Daniel A Nathan; pg130.

[95] *Saying It's So: A Cultural History of the Black Sox Scandal*, by Daniel A Nathan; pg7.

[96] *Burying the Black Sox*, by Gene Carney; pg 213.

[97] *Burying the Black Sox*, by Gene Carney; pg 214.

[98] *Burying the Black Sox*, by Gene Carney; pg 214.

[99] *Burying the Black Sox*, by Gene Carney; pg 91.

[100] *Saying It's So: A Cultural History of the Black Sox Scandal*, by Daniel A Nathan; pg203.

[101] *Saying It's So: A Cultural History of the Black Sox Scandal*, by Daniel A Nathan; pg119.

[102] *Saying It's So: A Cultural History of the Black Sox Scandal*, by Daniel A Nathan; pg130-131.

[103] *Burying the Black Sox*, by Gene Carney; pg 10.

[104] *Burying the Black Sox*, by Gene Carney; pg 41.

[105] *Burying the Black Sox*, by Gene Carney; pg 41.

[106] *Burying the Black Sox*, by Gene Carney; pg 73.

[107] *Burying the Black Sox*, by Gene Carney; pg 73.

[108] *Burying the Black Sox*, by Gene Carney; pg 73.

[109] *Burying the Black Sox*, by Gene Carney; pg 3.

Printed in the United States
119781LV00005B/58-246/P